# Get Ready, Read!

by Becky White

illustrated by
Vanessa Countryman

**Publisher**
Key Education Publishing Company, LLC
Minneapolis, Minnesota

## CONGRATULATIONS ON YOUR PURCHASE OF A KEY EDUCATION PRODUCT!

The editors at Key Education are former teachers who bring experience, enthusiasm, and quality to each and every product. Thousands of teachers have looked to the staff at Key Education for new and innovative resources to make their work more enjoyable and rewarding. We are committed to developing educational materials that will assist teachers in building a strong and developmentally appropriate curriculum for young children.

## PLAN FOR GREAT TEACHING EXPERIENCES WHEN YOU USE
## EDUCATIONAL MATERIALS FROM KEY EDUCATION PUBLISHING COMPANY, LLC

## Credits

Author: Becky White
Publisher: Sherrill B. Flora
Creative Director: Annette Hollister-Papp
Inside Illustrations: Vanessa Countryman
Project Director/Editor: Debra Pressnall
Copy Editor: Karen Seberg
Production: Sharon Thompson and
                Key Education Staff
Photo Credits: © Shutterstock

Key Education welcomes manuscripts and product ideas from teachers. For a copy of our submission guidelines, please send a self-addressed stamped envelope to:

**Key Education Publishing Company, LLC
Acquisitions Department
9601 Newton Avenue South
Minneapolis, Minnesota 55431**

## About the Author

Becky White has written more than 300 educational books for Key Education, Instructional Fair • T.S. Denison, Carson-Dellosa, Good Apple, Shining Star, The Education Center, Learning Works, and McGraw Hill. Her *Elementary Economics* (a six-book series for K-5), published by McGraw Hill, received *Learning* magazine's Teachers' Choice Gold Award for 2002. In 1980, Becky created a magazine called *Shining Star* for Good Apple Inc. and was the executive editor until 1993. Becky is a former elementary and middle school teacher and a graduate of California University at Long Beach. Becky White is the author of *Double Luck: Memoirs of a Chinese Orphan*, a true story of a boy's struggle to escape communist China and get to America. *Double Luck* was published by Holiday House in 2001 and won a Parents' Choice Gold Award for nonfiction.

## Copyright Notice

# Table of Contents

## Chapter IV
### More Short-Vowel Phonograms (Cont.)

## Chapter V
### Long-Vowel Phonograms
### (CVVC, CVCe, CVCC, CCVV & CCVCC Words)

## Chapter VI
### More Little Words: Variant Vowel,
### Diphthong, and *R*-Controlled Phonograms

# Introduction

Teaching children to read is important work, perhaps the most important work a teacher does. *Get Ready, Read!* provides a wealth of tools to help children get a strong start in discovering how to decode words. As beginning readers visually discriminate letter patterns and recognize word families (phonograms), they acquire knowledge about relationships between sounds and spelling. This skill is applied when reading meaningful text as children accurately recognize more words, thus increasing their reading fluency.

The logical place to begin teaching children to read is with what they already know—sounds. While still in the womb, babies hear sounds. By kindergarten, young children can say these sounds and put them into many words. Learning to read is simply an association of these sounds with symbols. But, where do you begin to cultivate these challenging connections? *Get Ready, Read!* provides a variety of activities that help students develop cognition in auditory and visual discrimination, learn to listen intently, and process written words. To make the teaching easier, each chapter includes the following:
  • Word-family lists
  • Clip art and reproducible word cards for a bulletin-board display
  • Phonemic awareness and word-decoding activities
  • Songs, games, and learning aids
  • Follow-up activities, such as word sorts, word-building exercises, and easy-to-play bingo games and/or a path game for additional decoding practice.
And, as a bonus, leaving up the bulletin-board displays transforms your classroom into a world of words!

## How to Use This Book

Listed below and on the following page are a variety of fun-filled ideas and helpful suggestions for ways to use some of the materials in this book.

### Word-Card Quick Tips
  • Copy on colorful card stock, cut out, and store a set of word cards for each chapter in a large manilla envelope to use on the bulletin-board word wall. Also, copy the word list for the chapter (pages 7, 42, 43, 82, 118, 119, 158, 159, 190, and 191) and staple it to the outside of the envelope to have as a convenient reference when working with students.
  • Have aids or older students copy on card stock, cut out, stack, and fasten a rubber band around a set of word cards that you have selected for each student. Store each set of cards in a small manilla envelope that has been personalized by the student.
  • Decorate a cardboard box where the students' envelopes may be filed when not in use.
  • Encourage students to take their envelopes home overnight for extra practice or have them search for those particular words in selected stories.

## A Dozen Songs Sung New!

Singing the letter sounds provides repetition that ordinarily would be tiresome and dull, but when silly lyrics are connected to a lively, familiar tune, a child will sing them again and again. Twelve simple, catchy songs are provided in *Get Ready, Read!* for you to use with children. Here are a few additional tips for teaching reading skills with songs:

- Turn the song into a guessing game. Students take turns singing a line as others identify the initial consonant or vowel sound they hear.
- Copy the words and send the songs home so that parents may sing along with their children.
- Assign song lines to individuals, pairs, or small groups of children. Practice and perform several songs for a kindergarten class or group of parents.
- After students learn each song, make a recording of their performance. At the end of the units, combine the recordings and burn a CD for each student. What a treasure they will have to cherish!

## Over 60 Circle Time Lessons and Games

When students are familiar with the rules of a game, play it again and again. Vary the games like this:
- Pair the students or form small groups and have children play as an independent guided-reading activity.
- Invite an older student to lead a small group of students in the game.
- Allow craft time for coloring and decorating picture game cards. Have each student place a set of game cards in a resealable plastic bag. Encourage them to take home their bags of cards to play with their families. For example: "Noisy Zoo Matchups" might be sent home with the rules for playing the five different games (see page 27).
- Have aids or older students decorate several extra sets of game cards to be placed in the literacy work station.

## Six Fabulous Bulletin-Board Word Walls

Once a bulletin-board word wall has been prepared by you and students have completed it, the board becomes much more than a visual, word-family motivator—it becomes the backdrop for a literacy work station and game hub. On a table under or near the board, you might arrange the following items:

- Cardboard box holding each child's manilla envelope of word cards
- Paper and pencils for writing short sentences (and later, stories) using the words found on the bulletin board
- Individual notebooks or stacks of paper stapled to form booklets, one for each student to create an illustrated dictionary (see pages 22 and 125 for reproducible booklet covers)
- Sets of game cards for the appropriate games, bingo boards and related materials, and assembled path games
- Extra copies of word picture cards to decorate along with crayons, paints, and/or markers
- Word-sorting and word-building activities for independent guided reading
- Picture books with limited text that children can use when hunting for other words that belong in certain word families; found words written on index cards and displayed
- Books and stories created by the students who use the word wall as a spelling resource

# Sounds and First Words

## Letters/ Phonemes

- ☐ b (/b/)
- ☐ c (/k/)
- ☐ c (/s/)
- ☐ d (/d/)
- ☐ f (/f/)
- ☐ g (/g/)
- ☐ g (/j/)
- ☐ h (/h/)
- ☐ j (/j/)
- ☐ k (/k/)
- ☐ l (/l/)
- ☐ m (/m/)
- ☐ n (/n/)
- ☐ p (/p/)
- ☐ qu (/kw/)
- ☐ r (/r/)
- ☐ s (/s/)
- ☐ s (/z/)
- ☐ t (/t/)
- ☐ v (/v/)
- ☐ w (/w/)
- ☐ x (/eks/)
- ☐ x (/ks/)
- ☐ y (/y/)
- ☐ z (/z/)

| | |
|---|---|
| a | am |
| an | as |
| at | I |
| if | in |
| is | it |
| on | ox |
| up | us |

# Noisy Zoo

b      d      f      g      h

j      k      l      m      n

## Bulletin-Board Word Wall

**Getting Ready:** You will need colorful colorful butcher paper, pencils, crayons, markers, scissors, construction paper, magazines, stapler, and art patterns on pages 9–21.

**Directions:**

1. Begin by covering the bulletin board with paper. Arrange the paper so that the top of this display can be reached by standing children if you would like them to point to objects.

2. Select the animals for the consonant sounds you will introduce. You may prefer to enlarge the art for the title and animals before making the reproductions on card stock. (Copy the title at 125% to make the lowercase letters about 3 in. [8 cm] in height.) Cut out the art along the dashed lines. Staple the title in the center of the top of the board. Color the animals as desired with markers and cut them out.

3. With a pencil, randomly divide the board into the desired number of spaces. Write a consonant letter in each section. Staple the related animal pictures in place or add them to the scene as the individual consonant sounds are introduced.

4. On a table near the board, place art supplies and a stapler for children to use to create additional decorations for the animal-park scene.

**Alternatively:** Children may delight in drawing other animals for the scene (see page 24).

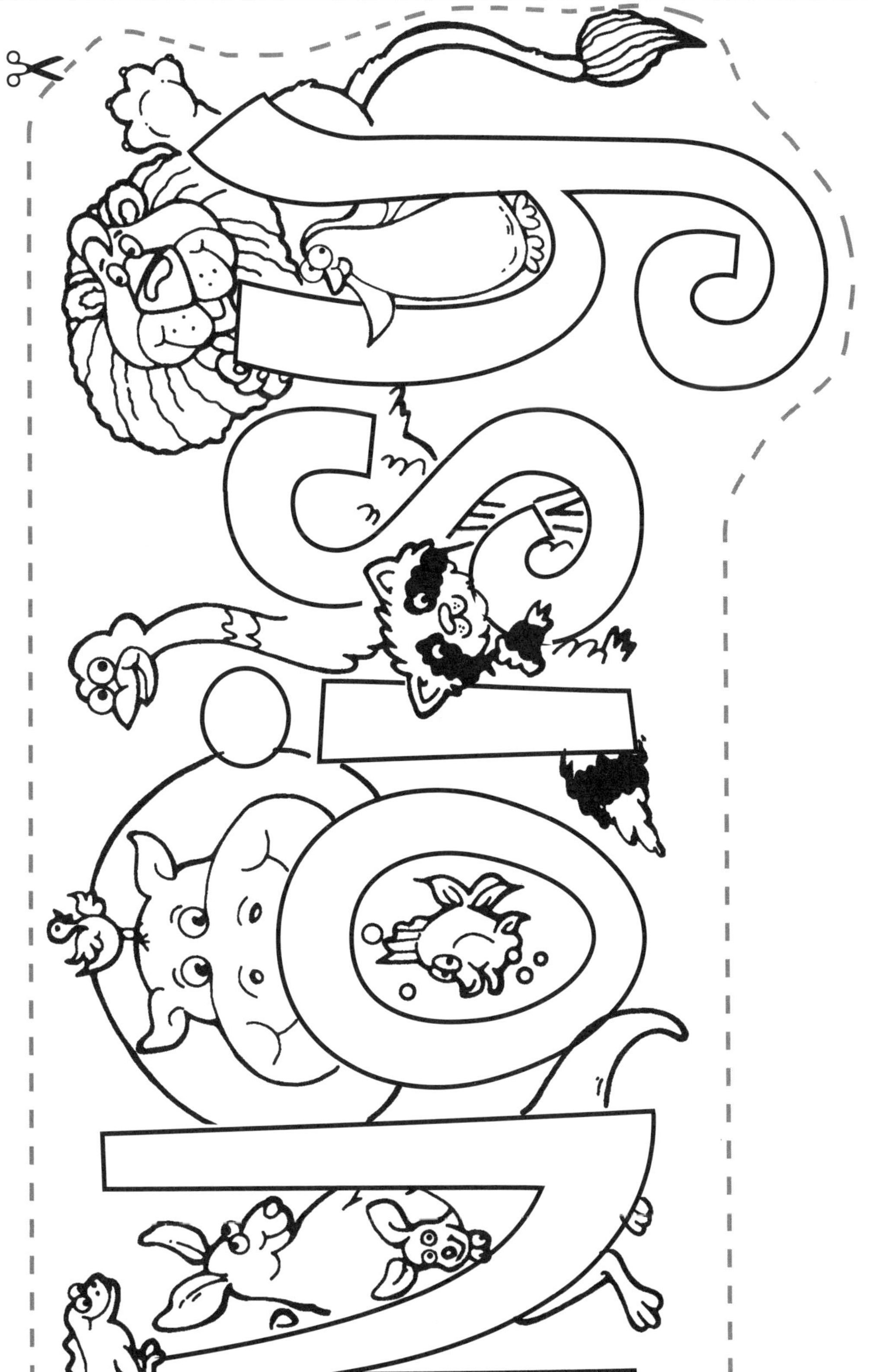
Noisy

**10**

/b/—bear and /d/—dog

/f/—fish and /g/—goat (hard G)

/h/—hippopotamus and /j/—jay

/k/—kangaroo and /l/—lion

/m/—moose and /n/—narwhal

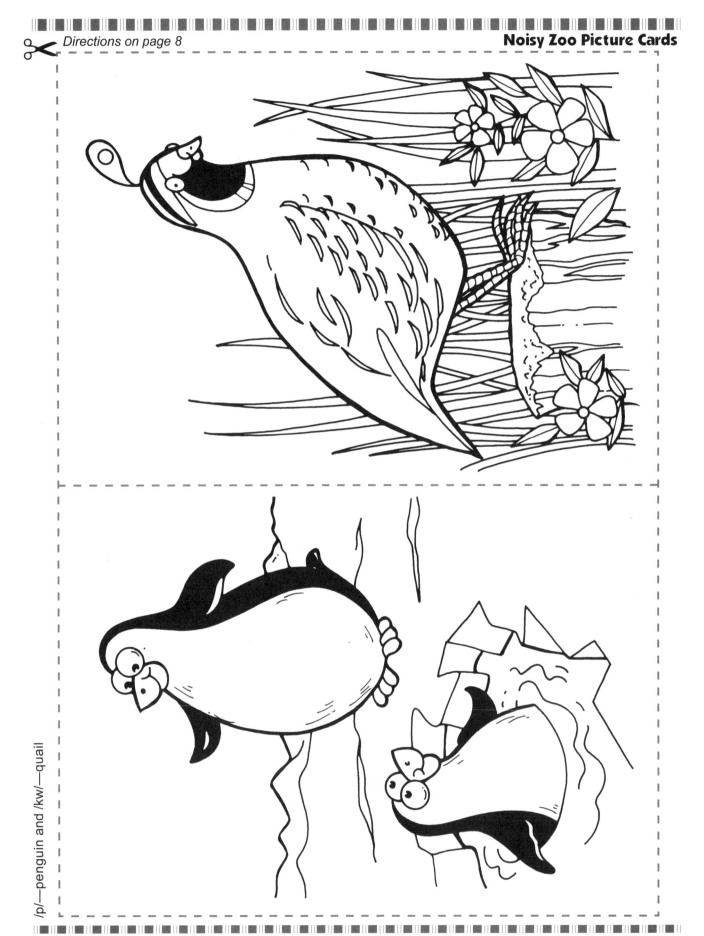

/p/—penguin and /kw/—quail

/r/—raccoon and /s/—seal

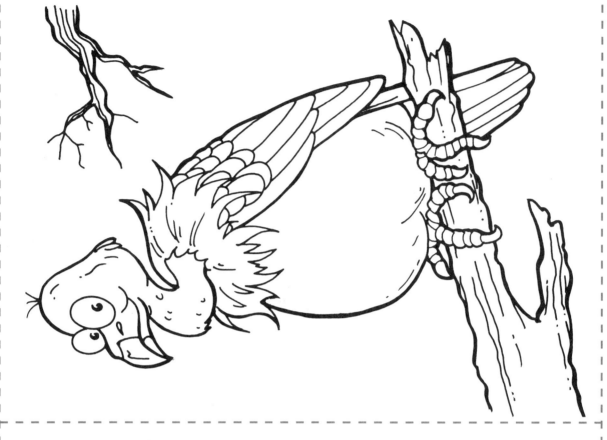

/t/—tiger and /v/—vulture

/w/—walrus and /y/—yak)

/ks/—fox (final consonant sound for X and /j/—giraffe (soft G)

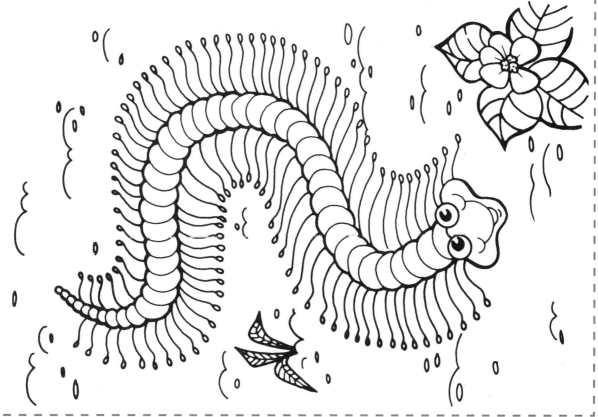

/s/—centipede (soft C) and /k/—cow (hard C)

booklet cover and /z/—zebra

# A Noisy Zoo for Beginning Letter Sounds

# Singing Letter Sounds

**Getting Ready:** Copy a set of picture cards on pages 11–22 onto card stock. Set aside the picture of the fox and the booklet cover. Select the letter sounds that are appropriate for children to practice identifying. Perhaps, your students are just learning to identify consonant sounds. Then, remove the pictures for the hard and soft C sounds (centipede and cow) and the soft G sound (giraffe).

**Directions:** Teach students the following song using the tune of "Zip-a-Dee-Doo-Dah." One at a time, hold up a picture card and sing a verse. Example for the letter *B*:

    *Lett-a* (letter) **B** *stands for /b/-/b/-/b/-/b/,*
    *My, oh, my,* **B** *has a wonderful sound.*
    *Plenty of* **B** *words headin' my way.*
    *Bip-a-bee-boo-bah, bip-a-bee-bay!*

Other verses:

    **C**—(hard *C* sound) *Kip-a-kee-koo-kah, kip-a-kee-kay!*
    **C**—(soft *C* sound) *Sip-a-see-soo-sah, sip-a-see-say!*
    **D**—*Dip-a-dee-doo-dah, dip-a-dee-day!*
    **F**—*Fip-a-fee-foo-fah, fip-a-fee-fay!*
    **G**—(hard *G* sound)—*Gip-a-gee-goo-gah, gip-a-gee-gay!*
    **G**—(soft *G* sound)—*Jip-a-jee-joo-jah, jip-a-jee-jay!*
    **H**—*Hip-a-hee-hoo-hah, hip-a-hee-hay!*
    **J**—*Jip-a-jee-joo-jah, jip-a-jee-jay!*
    **K**—*kip-a-kee-koo-kah, kip-a-kee-kay!*
    **L**—*Lip-a-lee-loo-lah, lip-a-lee-lay!*
    **M**—*Mip-a-mee-moo-mah, mip-a-mee-may!*
    **N**—*Nip-a-nee-noo-nah, nip-a-nee-nay!*
    **P**—*Pip-a-pee-poo-pah, pip-a-pee-pay!*
    **QU**—(blend *QU* sound) *Kwip-a-kwee-kwoo-kwah, kwip-a-kwee-kway!*
    **R**—*Rip-a-ree-roo-rah, rip-a-ree-ray!*
    **S**—(unvoiced *S* sound) *Sip-a-see-soo-sah, sip-a-see-say!*
    **T**—*Tip-a-tee-too-tah, tip-a-tee-tay!*
    **V**—*Vip-a-vee-voo-vah, vip-a-vee-vay!*
    **W**—*Wip-a-wee-woo-wah, wip-a-wee-way!*
    **Y**—*Yip-a-yee-yoo-yah, yip-a-yee-yay!*
    **Z**—*Zip-a-zee-zoo-zah, zip-a-zee-zay!*

# Mystery Letters

**Directions:** Use the song "Singing Letter Sounds" to play a guessing game. Choose a letter and say the sound it represents. See the following example.

    Teacher sings:    *What letter stands for /t/-/t/-/t/-/t/?*
    Students sing:    *My, oh, my,* **T** (shout the letter name) *has a wonderful sound.*
                      *Plenty of* **T** *words headin' my way.*
                      *Tip-a-tee-too-tah, tip-a-tee-tay!*

# The First Sound

**Directions:**

1. Begin by explaining how a letter or combination of letters represent speech sounds. Tell students that they are to listen for the sound at the beginning of each word, except for the word *fox*, in which the common sound for *X* is found at the end of the word.

2. Using the list below, introduce a few consonant sounds, working with the most common sounds first. Have students take turns repeating the names of animals, making the beginning sound in each word, and naming the initial letter. (The names of animals that begin with blends, such as *clam* and *snake*, should not be introduced at this time.)

3. As the names of animals are called out, list them on the board. Invite students to think of additional animals. Examples include the following:

    **B**—baboon, bear, beaver, bee, beetle, bird, bobcat, buffalo, butterfly
    **C**—(/k/) cat, cobra, cow; (/s/) centipede
    **D**—deer, dolphin, donkey, duck
    **F**—fawn, ferret, fish
    **G**—(/g/) goose, goat, gopher, gorilla, gull; (/j/) giraffe
    **H**—hamster, hen, horse, hyena
    **J**—jackrabbit, jaguar, jay, June bug
    **K**—kangaroo, koala
    **L**—ladybug, lamb, leopard, lizard, llama
    **M**—mice, moose, moth, mouse
    **N**—newt, narwhal
    **P**—parrot, peacock, pelican, penguin, pig, pigeon, porpoise
    **QU**—quail, queen bee
    **R**—rabbit, raccoon, ram, rattlesnake, raven, roadrunner, rooster
    **S**—salamander, seahorse, seal
    **T**—tiger, toucan, turkey
    **V**—vulture, vervet
    **W**—wallaby, walrus, weasel, wolf, woodpecker
    **X**—(/ks/) fox
    **Y**—yak, yellow jacket
    **Z**—zebra

**Optional:** Have students draw, color, cut out, and staple the animals in the appropriate locations on the bulletin board. (See page 8.)

# Consonant Safari

**Need:** Provide books and magazines along with pencils and small index cards.

**Directions:**

1. Determine which consonant letters children should identify in words. Write those letters on chart paper or poster board and display them near the Noisy Zoo bulletin board.

2. Have students look for words in books and magazines that begin with the featured consonants and write them on index cards. Display the words on the bulletin board.

# Going to the Bahamas

**Need:** Provide a backpack, bag, box, or other container with a name that begins with *B*.

**How to Play:**
1. Students sit in a circle.
2. The first student holds the backpack and says, "I am going to the **B**ahamas, and I am taking [name of object that begins with *B*]." Example: *bathing suit.* The student pretends to stuff the "bathing suit" into the backpack and then passes the backpack to the next student.
3. The second student says, "I am going to the Bahamas, and I am taking a *banana.*" Looking into the backpack, the student says, "[name of other student] is taking a bathing suit." Then, he pretends to put a banana into the backpack.
4. Continue around the circle, naming new *B* words. When a student forgets another student's word, the child who named it supplies the name of the object again.

**Culmination:** Have each student illustrate his *B* word on an index card and print the name of the object on another card. Place the picture and word cards on a table for students to match.

**Optional:** Play again, each time featuring a different initial consonant with the appropriate container and destination. Examples: *C*—case, California; *S*—suitcase or sack, Switzerland; *L*—luggage, Louisiana; and *P*—pouch, Portugal.

# Letter Bags

**Getting Ready:** As students are leaving for the day, assign the class a consonant letter. Explain that each student should return the next day with a paper bag containing an objecct whose name begins with that sound.

**Directions:** The next day, play the game Ten Guesses. Classmates ask 10 questions in an attempt to name what is in a student's bag. Guide students in asking questions that will narrow down the possibilities. Example questions:

1. Is it alive?
2. What color is it?
3. Does it have a smell?

4. What shape is it?
5. Does it belong to you?
6. In what room is it usually found?

# Serving Up Consonants

**Need:** Paper plates, black marker, objects whose names begin with the featured letters, container

**Getting Ready:**
1. Filling the entire space, use a black marker to print a consonant letter on each plate.
2. Place objects whose names begin with the featured letters in a large container.
3. Select four or five consonant paper plates and their corresponding objects for use in a literacy work station.

**Directions:** Have children match the objects whose names begin with the same sound by placing them on the corresponding paper plate. Continue until all objects have been sorted.

# Bingo Game: Noisy Zoo Sounds

**Getting Ready:** For each group of two players, copy the game cards on pages 28–32 onto colorful card stock. Cut out the picture and letter cards along the dashed lines. Discard the pictures of the cow and the cat and the letter *c* card. Then, sort the cards by placing the pictures shown in the middle column on each page in one resealable plastic bag. Place the remaining picture cards in a second resealable bag. Store the letter cards in a third plastic bag.

**Directions:**
1. Pair the students. Have each child choose a set of picture cards and place six pictures faceup on the table.
2. One at a time, draw a letter card from the plastic bag and then verbalize its phoneme.
3. Have students look at the pictures of the animals and think of their names. Each time a student hears the sound that matches the initial sound of an animal's name, the player flips that picture facedown.
4. The first player to flip over all six cards, calls out "It's a noisy zoo" and is declared the winner.

# Noisy Zoo Picture Riddles

**Getting Ready:** For each student, copy the game cards on pages 28–32 onto colorful card stock. Cut out the picture and letter cards along the dashed lines. Discard the letter cards.

**Directions:** The students hold their decks of cards in their laps. One at a time, ask a question that can be answered with a picture card. Have students hold up the corresponding pictures to answer the question.

Examples include the following:
Which name of an animal . . .
1. begins with /g/ and ends like *boat?* (goat)
2. begins with /k/ and ends like *rat?* (cat)
3. begins with /l/ and ends like *Sam?* (lamb)
4. begins with /d/ and ends like *hog?* (dog)
5. begins with /f/ and ends like *dish*? (fish)
6. begins with /s/ and ends like *meal?* (seal)
7. begins with /b/ and ends like *chair?* (bear)
8. begins with /h/ and ends like *force*? (horse)
9. begins with /m/ and ends like *house?* (mouse)
10. begins with /k/ and ends like *shoe?* (kangaroo)

**Optional:** Challenge students to look in books to learn more about the animals. Have each student choose two animals and then write riddles that offer facts about them. When finished, display the riddles in the literacy work station for other students to solve.

# Hunting for Words

**Getting Ready:** For each group of four players, you will need to provide a set of Noisy Zoo Matchups cards, paper, pencils, and small books with easy-to-read text. Copy the game cards on pages 28–32 onto colorful card stock. Cut out the picture and letter cards along the dashed lines. Discard the pictures of the koala and the kangaroo and the letter *k* card. Then, sort the cards by placing the pictures shown in the middle column on each page in one resealable plastic bag. Place the remaining picture cards in a second resealable bag. Store the letter cards in a third plastic bag.

**Directions:** Have the students form groups of four players. Within each group, pair the students. Give each team a plastic bag of picture cards. Have children take turns saying the names of the animals on the pictures and working together to find words that begin with the same letters. Encourage students to write those words on a sheet of paper. When finished, have the children share their words with the class.

# Noisy Zoo Memory Match

**Getting Ready:** For each group of two players, copy the game cards on pages 28–32 onto colorful card stock. Cut out the picture and letter cards along the dashed lines.

**Directions:**
1. Select the pairs of cards the students will use. They may match either pairs of pictures whose names begin with the same sound or picture card to initial consonant letter. Depending on the ability of students, choose eight or ten pairs of cards for children to match.
2. Place the cards facedown in four rows of four cards or five rows of four cards.
3. The first player selects two cards and turns them faceup. If a match has been found, the player keeps the cards and turns over two more cards. If no match is found, the cards are returned facedown to the playing area.
4. The second player takes a turn. Continue until all matching cards have been found.
5. The player who collects the most pairs of cards is declared the winner.

# Noisy Zoo Matchups

**Getting Ready:** For each group of two players, copy the game cards on pages 28–32 onto colorful card stock. Cut out the picture and letter cards along the dashed lines.

**How to Play:** For Level 1, have players set aside the letter cards and then scatter the picture cards faceup in the center of the playing area. The first player selects two cards and says the names of the pictures. If the names of the animals begin with the same sound, the player keeps the cards. If not, the cards are returned to the playing area. The second player now looks for two matching cards. The game continues in this manner until all matching pairs have been found. For Level 2, all cards are used. The players take turns selecting a letter card and then looking for two corresponding pictures whose names begin with the specified sound. Continue until all sets of matching cards are found.

*Directions on pages 26 and 27*

# Noisy Zoo Matchups

| | | |
|---|---|---|
| b |  |  |
| d |  |  |
| f |  |  |
| g |  |  |

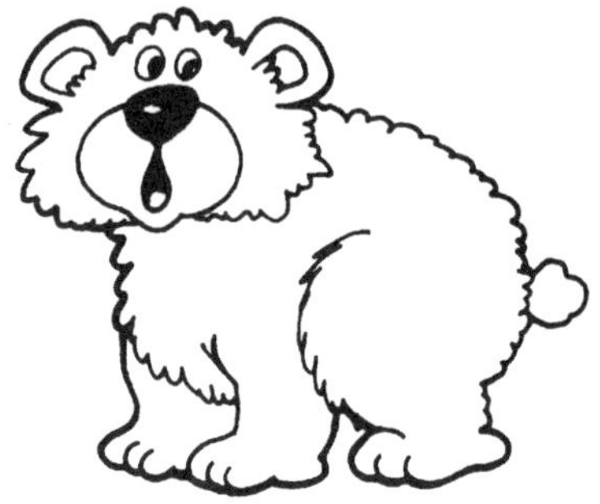

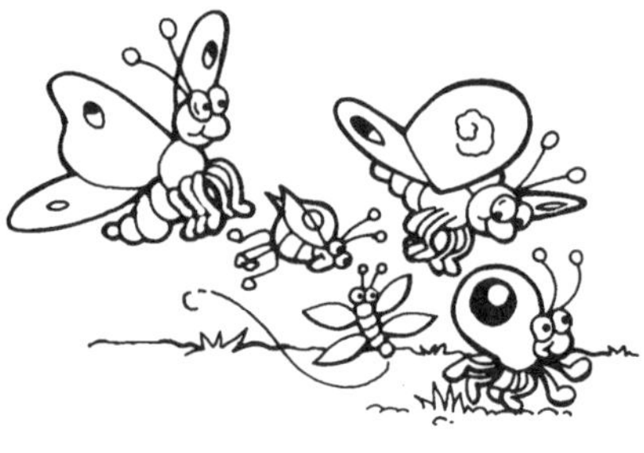

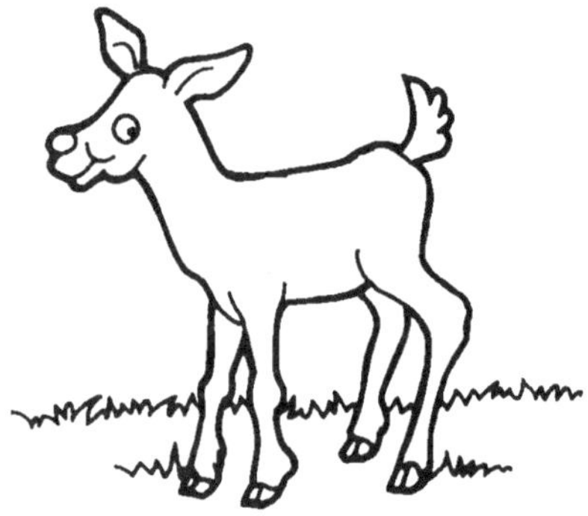

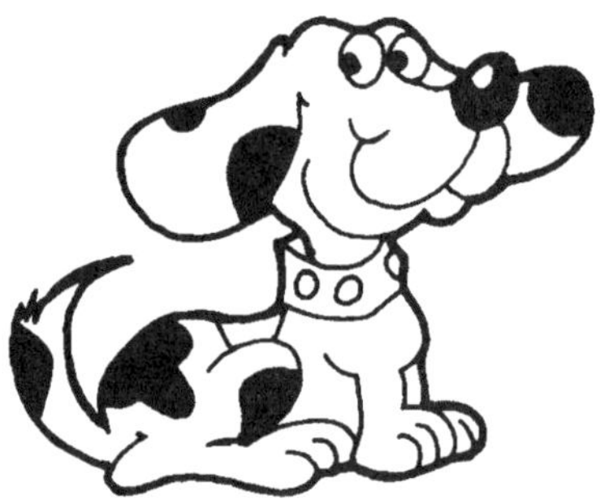

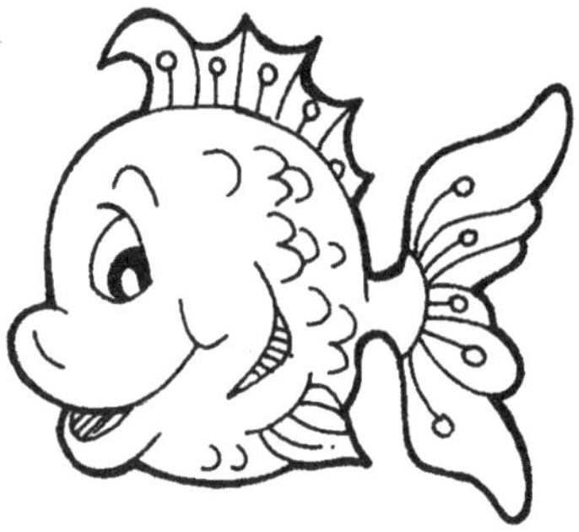

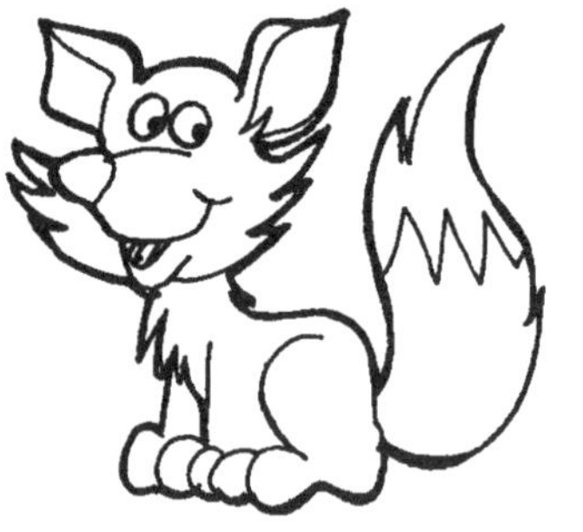

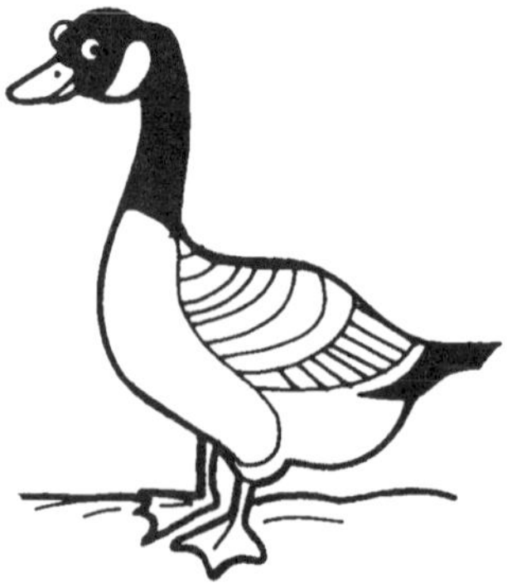

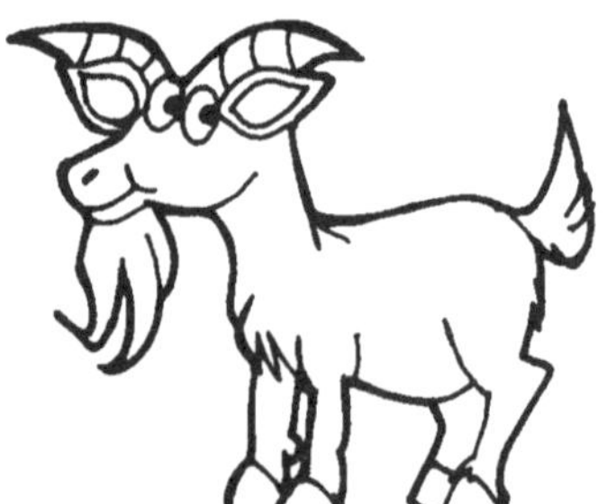

Pictures: bear, bugs and butterflies, deer, dog, fish, fox, goose, goat

# Noisy Zoo Matchups

| h | | |
| j | | |
| k | | |
| l | | |

Pictures: hippopotamus, horse, jay, jellyfish, kangaroo, koala, lion, lamb

# Noisy Zoo Matchups

| m | | |
|---|---|---|
| n | | |
| p | | |
| r | | |

Pictures: moose, mouse, newt, narwhal, penguin, porcupine, roadrunner, raccoon

# Noisy Zoo Matchups

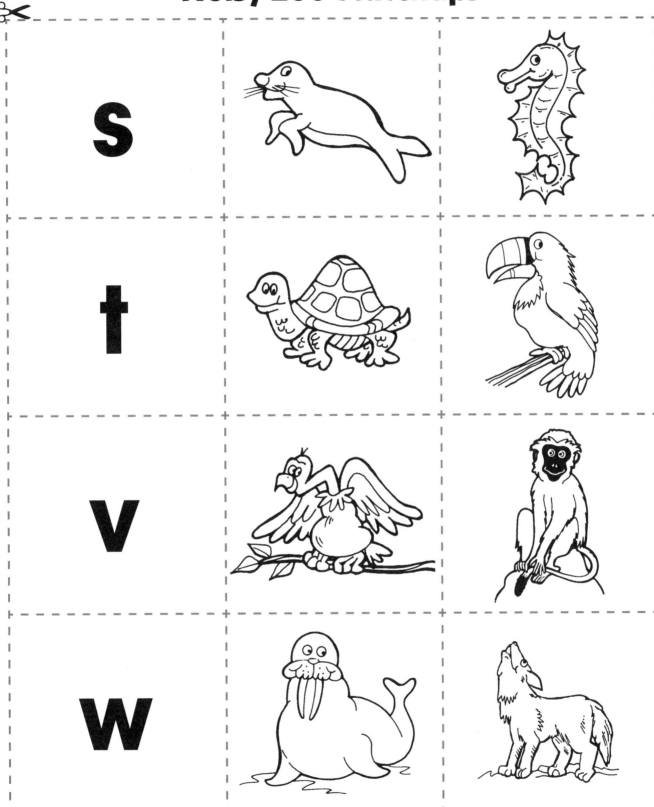

Pictures: seal, seahorse, turtle, toucan, vulture, vervet (monkey), walrus, wolf

*Directions on pages 26 and 27*

# Noisy Zoo Matchups

**y**

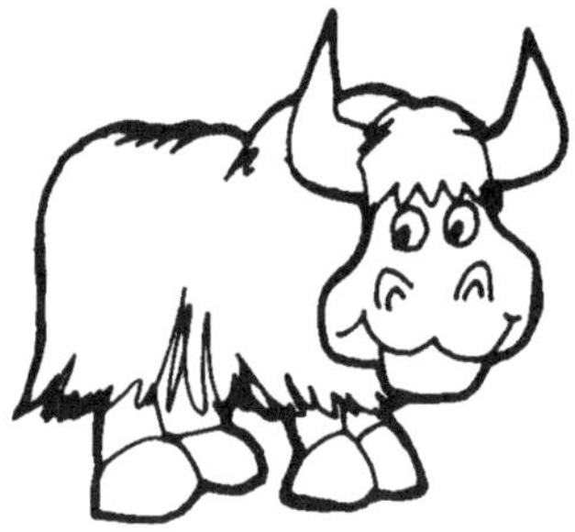

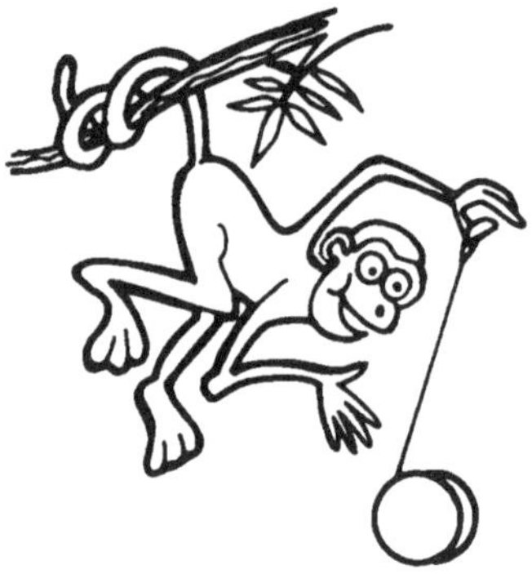

**z**

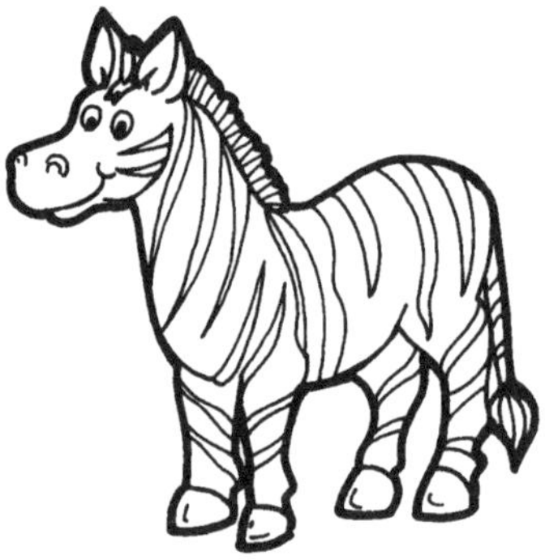

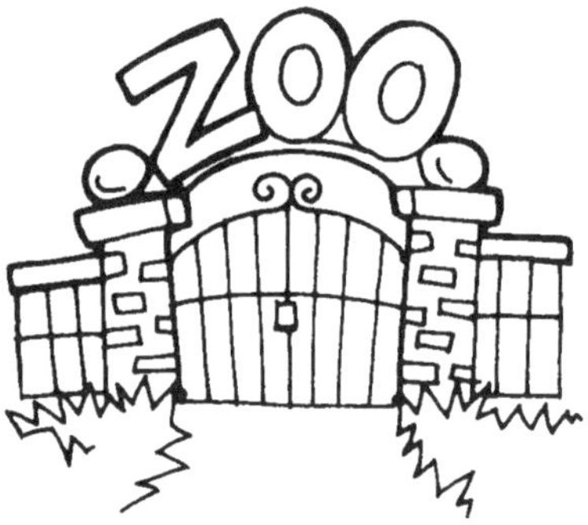

**qu**

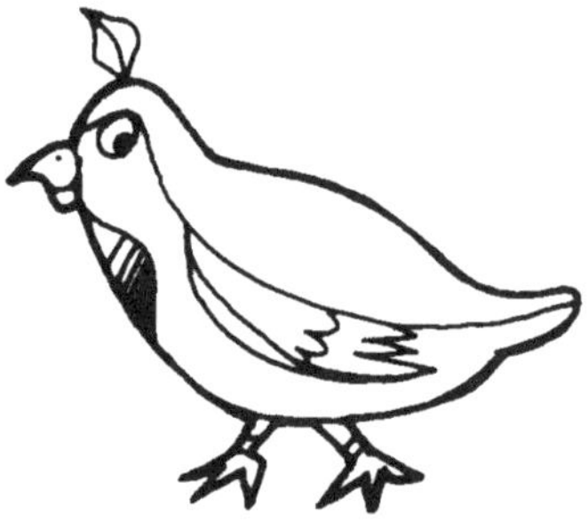

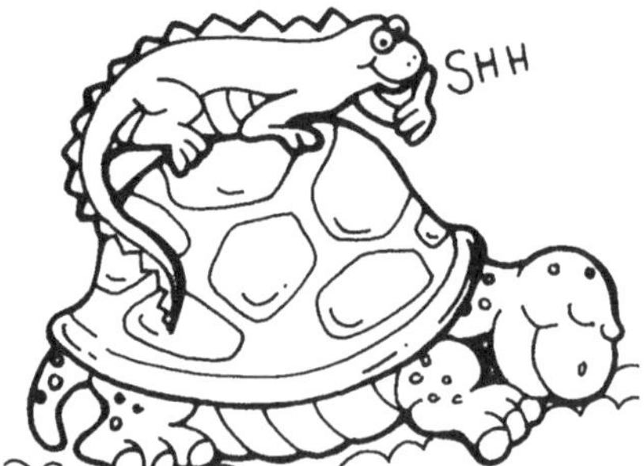

**c**

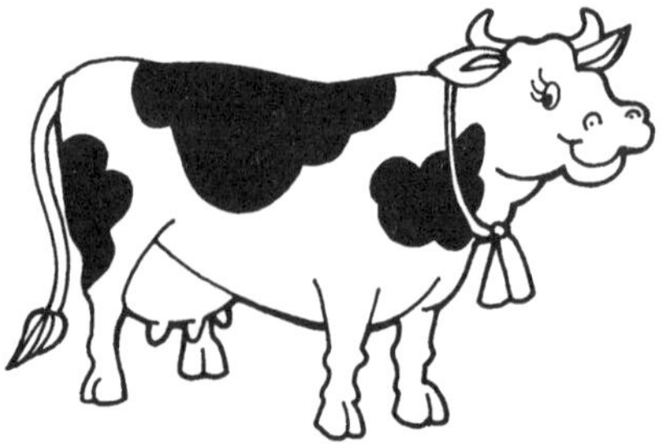

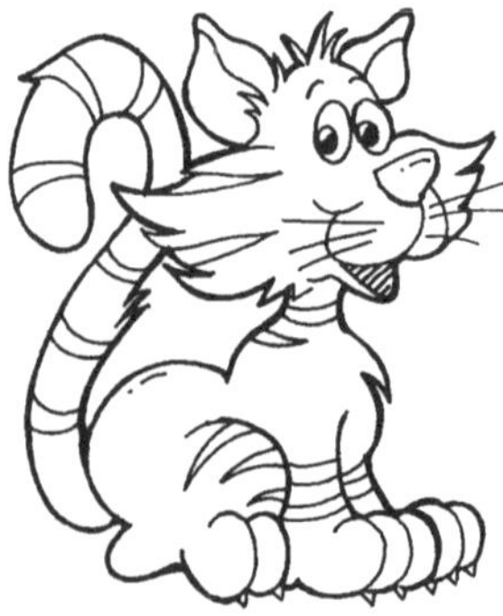

Pictures: yak, yo-yo (held by monkey), zebra, zoo, quail, quiet (as an action), cow, cat

# Sounds for C, G, and S

**Getting Ready:** Print the letters *Cc (/k/)*, *Cc (/s/)*, *Gg (/g/)*, *Gg (/j/)*, *Ss (/s/)*, and *Ss (/z/)* individually on small index cards. Gather pictures of the centipede, cow, giraffe, goat, and seal from the Noisy Zoo Picture Cards set (see pages 11–22).

**Directions:** Begin by choosing a word. Have students use two different voices—in a deep-pitched voice and a high voice—to say the word. Explain that some consonants stand for two different sounds. Introduce the two sounds for each of the three letters *C*, *G*, and *S*. Name the words below one at a time while showing the corresponding index card and picture card if available. Have students take turns naming the initial or final letter and making its related speech sound.

cow (*Cc*, /k/)     centipede (*Cc*, /s/)     seahorse (*Ss*, /s/)
cat (*Cc*, /k/)     giraffe (*Gg*, /j/)     goat (*Gg*, /g/)
bees (*Ss*, /z/)     gorilla (*Gg*, /g/)     seal (*Ss*, /s/)

# Letter Q Never Walks Alone

**Directions:** Begin by explaining that the letter *Q* is almost always followed by the letter *U*. The letters *QU* represent the same sounds used for the letters *K* and *W*. Say /kw/. Pair students and have them look in books and find five *QU* words. Invite students to share those words during large-group time.

# Mr. X Steals Sounds

**Directions:** Begin by explaining to children that most consonants represent one particular sound. However, at the beginning of a word, the letter *X* can either say its own name (/eks/) as in *x-ray*, or it can represent the sound /z/ as in *xylophone*. In addition, when the letter appears at the end of a word such as *fox*, *X* stands for the sound of two letters. See who can figure out the two letters (/ks/) that make that sound for *X*. Then, have students draw cartoons of Mr. *X* saying "EKS," "Z," and "KS."

# Bingo Game: Noisy Zoo Letters

**Getting Ready:** Copy the bingo boards on pages 34–36 onto colorful card stock for each group of six students. Cut apart the boards along the dashed lines. To prepare the calling cards, copy page 37 onto card stock for each group and cut apart the pictures. Give each student nine game markers.

**Directions:** Shuffle the picture cards. Choose someone to be the "caller." Drawing one card at a time, the caller announces the name of the animal in the picture. Each time students hear the beginning sound for one of the letters shown on their boards, they cover that letter with a marker. The first player to cover all squares on a board calls out "It's a noisy zoo" and is declared the winner.

# Noisy Zoo Letters

Bingo Board #2

| s | d | l |
|---|---|---|
| v | f | y |
| k | n | h |

# Noisy Zoo Letters

Bingo Board #1

| m | t | g |
|---|---|---|
| n | b | w |
| j | z | r |

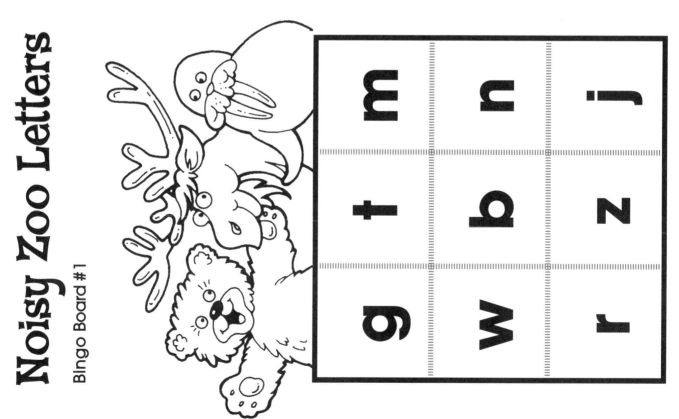

# Noisy Zoo Letters
### Bingo Board #4

| l | z | p |
|---|---|---|
| y | j | f |
| b | v | s |

# Noisy Zoo Letters
### Bingo Board #3

| g | w | m |
|---|---|---|
| r | h | z |
| n | d | t |

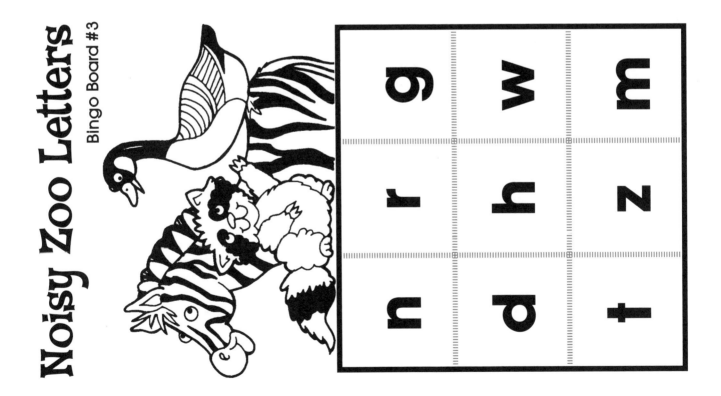

# Noisy Zoo Letters

*Bingo Board #6*

| h | v | m |
|---|---|---|
| w | d | k |
| p | t | j |

# Noisy Zoo Letters

*Bingo Board #5*

| p | k | f |
|---|---|---|
| r | g | s |
| b | y | l |

# Reading Itty-Bitty Words

**Getting Ready:** On the board, list the following words in two sets: *a, I, an, at, in, it, on,* and *am, ax, if, up.* Distribute a copy of the Noisy Zoo Picture Cards (see pages 11–22) to each child for the letters *f, m, n, p, t,* and *x.*

**Directions:**
1. Begin by explaining that words are treasures. Each word that we learn to read opens our world a bit wider. Say, "The more words you can read, the more you can learn."
2. Read aloud the list of words in the first group. Then, say the two-letter words in random order with "stretched" speech sounds to help students hear the phonemes in the words. As each word is pronounced, have students decide if the final sound is /n/ or /t/ and then hold up their corresponding Noisy Zoo Picture Cards.
3. Direct students to look at the words on the board. Encourage them to point to the words that end either with the letter *n* or *t.*
4. Have students take turns reading the words one at a time in the first set as you point to them.
5. Repeat the steps by practice reading the second set of words with children and matching the picture cards for *f, m, p,* and *x* (fox) to the final sounds in the words.

# Buzzin' About the Letter S

**Getting Ready:** On the board, list the words *as, is,* and *us.* Copy the buzzin' bee on page 39 for each child. Cut out each bee and glue it to a craft stick so that it can "fly."

**Directions:**
1. Give each child a bee on a craft stick. Read the three words listed on the board to the students. Have them listen carefully to discover which two words end with the same sound (*as* and *is*). Tell the students to make a "buzzing" sound when they hear that speech sound at the end of a word. Say the words again with stretched sounds as you move a finger under the letters. Then, read the words aloud in a normal manner.
2. Have students listen to other words that end either with the /z/ or /s/ sound. Examples include *his, bees, bats, ours, cars, says, bikes, news, hers, has, dolls, trucks, marbles,* and *does.* Each time children hear the final consonant sound /z/, have them move their bees as if "flying."

# Simon Says

**Getting Ready:** Copy the word cards (First Words) on page 7 onto colorful card stock for each student. (*You may prefer to enlarge the words before copying them.*) Cut out the cards and put a paper clip on each set. List the two-letter words on the board.

**How to Play:** Distribute a set of cards to each child. One at a time, hold up a two-letter word card. Say, "Simon says [followed by a direction]."

**Examples:** Put the word *am* on your arm; wave *an* in the air; hold *in* in your hand; hold up the word *up*; point the word *us* at me, put the word *on* on your lap, and so on.

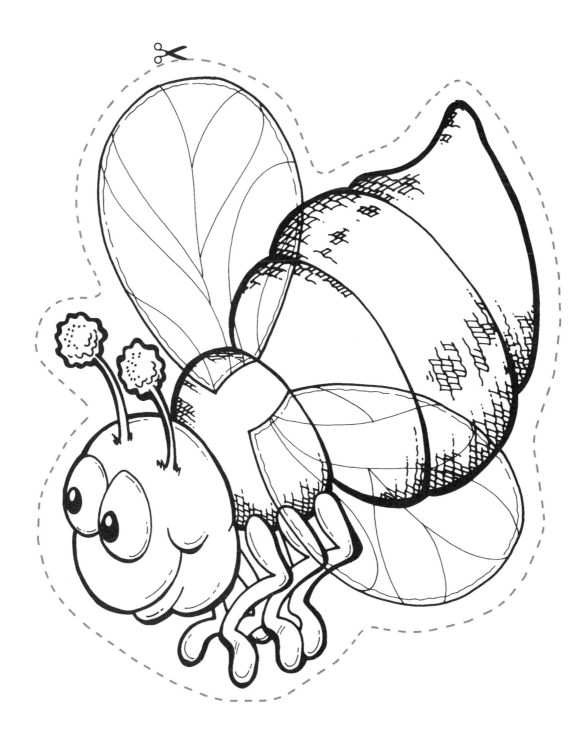

# Listen Up for Sounds

**Getting Ready:** Copy the Noisy Zoo Picture Cards for the letters *b, c, d, f, g, h, j, l, m, n, p, r, s, t, v, w, y,* and *z* (see pages 11–22) for each child. Store each set of cards in a resealable plastic bag. Make one copy of the word list on page 41 for the activity.

**Directions:**

1. Select three to five animal cards from the set for the children to use. Direct children to find those pictures and place them faceup on a flat surface. Choose words from the list on page 41 that either begin or end with those selected sounds. For example, the picture cards could be for the letters *d, m, p, r,* and *s.*

2. Say the chosen word (e.g., *red*). Stretch the sounds in the word as you say it a second time. (e.g., /rrrrreeed/). Ask the children to think about the beginning sound in the word. Have them find their pictures whose names begin with the same sound and hold them up for you to see (e.g., raccoon). Say the word again, this time separating the phonemes (e.g., /r/-/e/-/d/) and ask children to think about the final sound in the word. Say: "What sound do you hear? Which picture stands for that sound?" (Answer: /d/ as in *dog*)

3. Continue the game as time allows. Check the boxes on the word list of those words that are used.

4. Play again on another day with a different selection of pictures and words.

# Celebrate Learning to Read

**Directions:** Teach students the song "I've Been Working on My Reading," sung to the tune of "I've Been Working on the Railroad."

*I've been workin' on my reading,*
*All the live long day.*
*I've been workin' on my reading,*
*Just to pass the* [name of grade; e.g., first grade].
*Don't you know the sounds of letters?*
*Some stand for two or three.*
*When we put them all together,*
*Then we all can read.*
*Study 'til we know. (Sing twice.)*
*Study 'til we know how to read.*
*Study 'til we know. (Sing twice.)*
*Study 'til we can read.*

# Word List for Listen Up for Sounds

| | | | | | | |
|---|---|---|---|---|---|---|
| ☐ bad | ☐ dim | ☐ hog | ☐ mop | ☐ pup | ☐ run | ☐ van |
| ☐ bag | ☐ dip | ☐ hop | ☐ mud | ☐ rag | ☐ sad | ☐ vet |
| ☐ ban | ☐ dog | ☐ hot | ☐ mug | ☐ ram | ☐ sag | ☐ wag |
| ☐ bat | ☐ dot | ☐ hug | ☐ nab | ☐ ran | ☐ sap | ☐ wet |
| ☐ bed | ☐ dug | ☐ hum | ☐ net | ☐ rat | ☐ sat | ☐ wig |
| ☐ bet | ☐ fan | ☐ hut | ☐ nip | ☐ red | ☐ sip | ☐ win |
| ☐ bib | ☐ fed | ☐ jab | ☐ nod | ☐ rib | ☐ six | ☐ wit |
| ☐ bid | ☐ fib | ☐ jam | ☐ nut | ☐ rig | ☐ sob | ☐ yam |
| ☐ big | ☐ fig | ☐ jet | ☐ pan | ☐ rim | ☐ sun | ☐ yet |
| ☐ bin | ☐ fin | ☐ jig | ☐ pat | ☐ rip | ☐ tap | ☐ yip |
| ☐ bit | ☐ fit | ☐ jot | ☐ peg | ☐ rob | ☐ ten | ☐ zip |
| ☐ bog | ☐ fix | ☐ jug | ☐ pen | ☐ rod | ☐ top | |
| ☐ bud | ☐ fog | ☐ kin | ☐ pet | ☐ rot | ☐ tub | |
| ☐ bug | ☐ fun | ☐ kit | ☐ pod | ☐ rug | ☐ tug | |
| ☐ bus | ☐ gab | ☐ lab | | | | |
| ☐ cab | ☐ gag | ☐ lag | | | | |
| ☐ cat | ☐ gap | ☐ let | | | | |
| ☐ cob | ☐ gas | ☐ lid | | | | |
| ☐ cod | ☐ get | ☐ lip | | | | |
| ☐ cot | ☐ had | ☐ log | | | | |
| ☐ cub | ☐ ham | ☐ mad | | | | |
| ☐ cut | ☐ has | ☐ man | | | | |
| ☐ dab | ☐ hat | ☐ map | | | | |
| ☐ dad | ☐ hen | ☐ mat | | | | |
| ☐ den | ☐ hid | ☐ men | | | | |
| ☐ did | ☐ him | ☐ met | | | | |
| ☐ dig | ☐ hip | ☐ mix | | | | |

# Short-Vowel Phonograms
## (CVC Words)

### Short "a" Families

*Note*: Due to differences in dialects, certain word families, such as the -og family, may not have short-vowel sounds when spoken in your area.

| -ab | -ad | -ag | -am | -an | -at |
|-----|-----|-----|-----|-----|-----|
| cab* | bad* | bag* | ham* | can* | bat |
| dab | dad* | lag | jam* | fan* | cat* |
| gab* | had* | rag* | yam* | man | fat |
| jab | mad | sag | | pan* | hat* |
| lab* | sad | tag | **-ap** | ran | mat |
| nab | | wag* | cap | tan | pat |
| tab | | | map* | van | rat* |
| | | | nap* | | sat |
| | | | rap* | | |
| | | | sap | | |

### Short "e" Families

| -ed | -eg | -en | -et |
|-----|-----|-----|-----|
| bed* | beg* | den | bet |
| fed* | keg | hen* | get |
| led | leg* | men | jet* |
| red* | peg* | pen* | let |
| | | ten* | met* |
| | | | net |
| | | | pet |
| | | | set* |
| | | | vet |
| | | | wet |
| | | | yet |

## Vowel Sounds Picture Key

short "a"          short "e"

short "i"          short "o"

short "u"

*The word is already printed on a card (see pages 51–55).*

## Short "i" Families

| -ib | -id | -ig | -im | -in | -ip | -it | -ix |
|-----|-----|-----|-----|-----|-----|-----|-----|
| bib* | bid | big* | dim* | bin | dip* | bit* | fix* |
| fib* | did* | dig* | him* | fin* | hip | fit | mix* |
| rib* | hid* | fig | rim* | kin | lip* | hit* | six* |
| | lid* | pig* | | pin* | rip | kit | |
| | rid | rig | | tin | sip | lit | |
| | | wig | | win* | tip | pit | |
| | | | | | yip | sit* | |
| | | | | | zip* | wit | |

## Short "o" Families

| -ob | -od | -og | -op | -ot | -ox |
|-----|-----|-----|-----|-----|-----|
| cob* | cod | dog* | cop | cot* | box |
| rob* | nod* | fog* | hop* | dot | fox |
| sob* | pod* | hog | mop* | got* | |
| | rod* | jog | top* | hot* | |
| | | log* | | jot | |
| | | | | not | |
| | | | | pot | |

## Short "u" Families

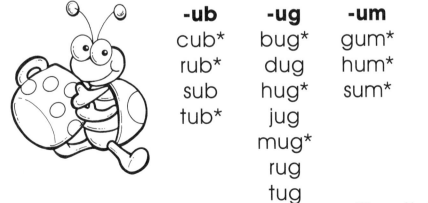

| -ub | -ug | -um | -un | -up | -ut |
|-----|-----|-----|-----|-----|-----|
| cub* | bug* | gum* | bun | cup* | but* |
| rub* | dug | hum* | fun* | pup* | cut* |
| sub | hug* | sum* | run* | sup* | gut |
| tub* | jug | | sun* | | hut* |
| | mug* | | | | nut |
| | rug | | | | rut |
| | tug | | | | |

*The word is already printed on a card (see pages 51–55).*

# Shop for Sounds

_an — can, fan
_ab — cab, lab
_ip — dip, lip, zip

_et — jet, met, set
_ug — bug, hug
_ut — cut, hut

fix, cub, box
cap, bed
_ob — rob, sob
_ot — cot, got

# Bulletin-Board Word Wall

**Getting Ready:** You will need colorful butcher paper, colorful card stock, markers, scissors, stapler, and patterns on pages 45–55.

**Directions:**

1. Begin by covering the bulletin board with paper. Arrange the paper so that the top of this display can be reached by standing children if you would like them to point to words.

2. Copy the title and decorative art on pages 45–49 onto colorful card stock. You may prefer to enlarge certain pieces of art before making the reproductions. (Copy the title at 125% to make the lowercase letters about 3 in. [8 cm] in height.) Color the art as desired with markers and then cut out the individual pieces. Staple the title in the center of the top of the board. Use a marker to divide the space into three or five shelves.

3. Select the phonograms you will introduce and then copy the needed number of shapes on pages 49 and 50 onto colorful card stock for displaying the word families. Also, copy and cut out a set of the word cards on pages 51–55.

4. Place all materials on a table by the board and then add the pieces to the display as new words are introduced during classroom activities.

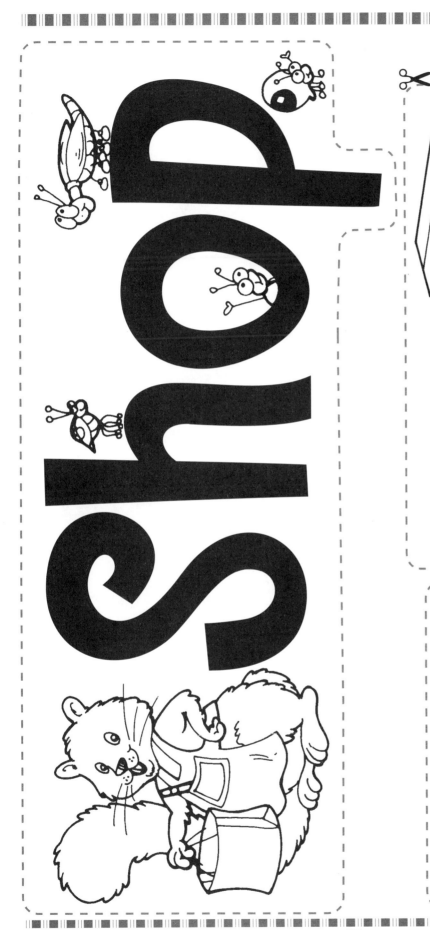

Sounds

# Short "e" Sound

# Short "a" Sound

## Short "o" Sound

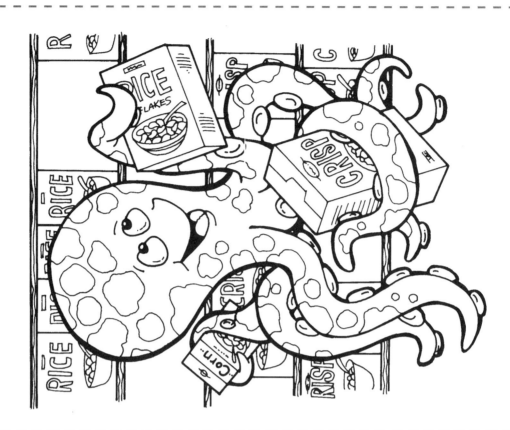

## Short "i" Sound

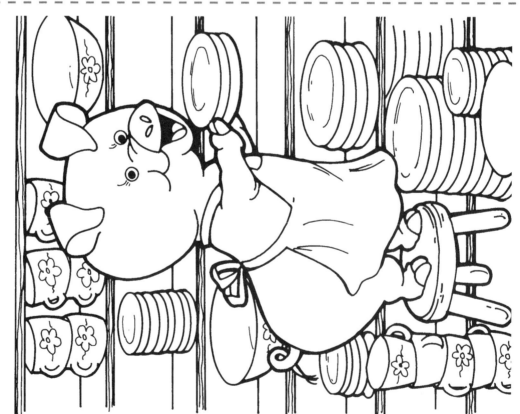

# Short "u" Sound

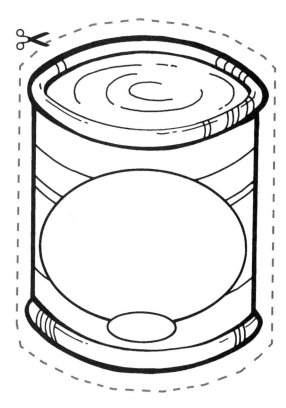

| cab | gab | lab |
|-----|-----|-----|
| bad | dad | had |
| bag | rag | wag |
| can | fan | pan |
| cat | hat | rat |
| map | nap | rap |

| ham | jam | yam |
| --- | --- | --- |
| beg | leg | peg |
| hen | pen | ten |
| jet | met | set |
| bed | fed | red |
| bib | fib | rib |

| did | hid | lid |
| :---: | :---: | :---: |
| big | dig | pig |
| dim | him | rim |
| fin | pin | win |
| dip | lip | zip |
| bit | hit | sit |

| fix | mix | six |
| --- | --- | --- |
| cob | rob | sob |
| nod | pod | rod |
| dog | fog | log |
| hop | mop | top |
| cot | got | hot |

| cub | rub | tub |
| --- | --- | --- |
| bug | hug | mug |
| cup | pup | sup |
| gum | hum | sum |
| fun | run | sun |
| but | cut | hut |

# "At" Is the Word

**Getting Ready:** Print the following numbered sentences on the board.

1. Pat the rat.
2. The rat has a hat.
3. The cat is on the mat.
4. The rat sat in a vat.
5. The bat is fat.

**Directions:**

1. Begin by reviewing the little word *at*. Say the short /a/ sound followed by the /t/ sound.
2. Print the word *at* on the board. Then, write *bat*. Ask, "Who can sound out this word?"
3. One word at a time, write a list of -*at* words: *bat, cat, fat, hat, mat, pat, rat,* and *sat*. Encourage students to take turns reading the words out loud.
4. Randomly read aloud the sentences on the board. Have students indicate which one they hear by a show of fingers for the corresponding number of the sentence.

**Culmination:** Select the -*at* words you would like to add to the bulletin-board word wall and print them on small index cards that have been cut in half. Label one of the cans with the letters -*at*. The words *cat, hat,* and *rat* are provided on page 51. Alternatively, have children print the -*at* words on the can labels and add them to the bulletin board.

# If It's a Word and You Know It

**Getting Ready:** On chart paper, list the following words: *am, an, as, is, it, up,* and *us*.

**Directions:**

1. Read aloud the list of two-letter words.
2. Teach students the song "If It's a Word and You Know It," sung to the tune of "If You're Happy and You Know It!" As a class, sing the song, naming the listed two-letter words.

   *If it's a word and you know it, say it now. (Say the word twice.)*
   *If it's a word and you know it, say it now. (Say the word twice.)*
   *If it's a word and you know it, then you really ought to say it.*
   *If it's a word and you know it, say it now. (Say the word twice.)*

3. On chart paper, one word at a time, print the following words: *ham, jam, ram, yam, can, fan, man, pan, ran, tan, van, gas, has, bit, fit, hit, kit, pit, sit,* and *wit*. As a class, sing the song, naming the listed three-letter words.

**Culmination:** Select the -*am* words you would like to add to the "Shop for Sounds" bulletin-board word wall and print them on small index cards that have been cut in half. Label one of the cans with the letters -*am*. The words *ham, jam,* and *yam* are provided on page 52. Alternatively, have children print the -*am* words on the can labels and add them to the bulletin board.

# Short *i* or Short *o* Sound?

**Getting Ready:** On the board, list the following words: *him\*, zip\*, got\*, rod\*, fix\*, mop\*, fig, hot\*, mix\*, sob\*, tin, hop\*, did\*, dip\*, fib\*, cop, win\*, rob\*, fox, wig, fin\*, lit, yip, box,* and *six\*.*

**Directions:**
1. Randomly say each word.
2. Have students indicate which short vowel they hear by pointing their index fingers for the short *i* sound and using index fingers and thumbs to make circles for the short *o* sound.
3. After the group has indicated the vowel, choose a student to come forward and point to the corresponding word.

**Culmination:** Select the words you would like to add to the "Shop for Sounds" bulletin-board word wall and print them on small index cards that have been cut in half. Label the word families on the appropriate shapes and display them with the words. (*Note*: Words above marked with an asterisk are provided on pages 52–55.)

# What Vowel's in the Middle?

**Getting Ready:** On the board, list the following words: *rap\*, sag, bag\*, bud, bug\*, mug\*, ten\*, rag\*, run\*, dad\*, tug, gab\*, rub\*, had\*, tub\*, sum\*, hot\*, sap, hum\*, jug, yet, set\*, bid, bin, dig\*, pet, dog\*,* and *net.*

**Directions:** Teach students the song "What Vowel's in the Middle," sung to the tune of "The Farmer in the Dell." Choose a word from the list and read it aloud. Repeat as time and interest allow.

| | |
|---|---|
| Teacher sings: | *What sound do you hear first?* |
| | *What sound do you hear first?* |
| Students sing: | **/B/ - /b/ - /b/ - /b/ - /b/ - /b/** |
| | **/B/** *is the first sound.* |
| Teacher sings: | *What vowel's in the middle?* |
| | *What vowel's in the middle?* |
| Students sing: | **/A/ - /a/ - /a/ - /a/ - /a/ - /a/** |
| | Sing the short *a* sound as in <u>apple</u>.) |
| | *Short* **a** *is in the middle.* |
| Teacher sings: | *What sound do you hear last?* |
| | (Continue as above.) |
| Teacher sings: | *What letters spell the word?* |
| | *What letters spell the word?* |
| Students sing: | **B - a - g, b - a - g** |
| | *That's how we all spell* **bag**. |

**Culmination:** Follow the directions provided in the previous activity for the bulletin-board word wall.

# Where's That Sound?

**Getting Ready:** On the board, list the following words: *sad, pen\*, hip, pod\*, sip, cob\*, wag\*, beg\*, bet, dim\*, sun\*, tug, den, jab, keg, met\*, jog, peg\*, lab, lag, fun\*, get, rip, cod,* and *log\*.*

**Directions:** Have students stand to play this action game. Choose one of the short vowel words listed on the board and say it aloud. Then, say one of the letter sounds in that word. Ask, "Is the sound at the beginning, middle, or end of the word?" Students indicate the location by touching top of head (beginning), tummy (middle), or feet (end). Finally, underline the letter or vowel in the word that stands for that sound. Continue in the same manner with other words as time and interest allow.

**Culmination:** Select the words you would like to add to the "Shop for Sounds" bulletin-board word wall and print them on small index cards that have been cut in half. Label the word families on the appropriate shapes and display them with the words. (*Note:* Words above marked with an asterisk are provided on pages 52–55.)

# Hide-and-Seek Words

**Getting Ready:** On the board, list the following words: *bad\*, cab\*, dab, lab, map\*, nap\*, bed, hen\*, let, men, red\*, vet, bib\*, big\*, hid\*, lid\*, lip\*, mix\*, nip, pig\*, pin\*, rib\*, rid, rig, rim\*, tip, cot\*, not, fog\*, got\*, top\*, jot, pot, nod\*, bun, cup\*, but\*, cut\*, dug, gut, hug\*, rug,* and *sub.* On individual slips of paper, write one of the words. While students are away from the classroom, hide the slips of paper around the room.

**Directions:** When students return, let everyone search for the words. When all of the words have been found, have students take turns reading them aloud.

**Culmination:** Follow the directions provided in the previous activity for the bulletin-board word wall.

# Roll and Read Three-Letter Words

**Getting Ready:** For each group of two to four players, you will need three letter dice, scissors, and glue. Copy the dice patterns and word list on pages 59 and 60 onto colorful card stock. Cut out the dice patterns along the dashed lines. Fold each pattern along the solid lines to form a cube shape. Glue the tabs as indicated on the dice.

**How to Play:** In each group, the players take turns rolling all three of the dice. The player then attempts to spell a word(s) with the vowel and two consonants indicated and writes the letters on a sheet of paper. Example: *u, g, m—mug, gum.* The lowercase *d* can also be used as the letter *p.* The asterisk on the vowel cube can be any vowel the student wishes to name. Students may also refer to the word list on page 59 when trying to build words. At the end of the predetermined time or specified number of rounds, the player with the most words is declared the winner.

**Optional:** Roll the dice five times and record the letters indicated by writing them on paper. Use the specified letters to write new words. Encourage students to refer to the bulletin-board word wall as a resource if needed.

## Roll and Read Three-Letter Words

**Examples include the following words:**

b:  ban, bat, bet, bin, bit, bum, bun, bus, but
c:  can, cat, cot, cut
d:  den, dim, dot
f:  fan, fat, fin, fit, fun
g:  gas, gem, get, got, gum, gun, gut
h:  ham, has, hat, hen, him, his, hit, hot, hum, hut
j:  jab, jig, job, jog, jug
l:  lab, lad, lag, led, leg, lid, log, lug
m:  man, men, mug
n:  nab, nag
p:  pan, pat, pen, pet, pot
s:  sad, sag, sap, sip, sob, sub
t:  tab, tag, tap, tip, top, tub, tug

**Die A**

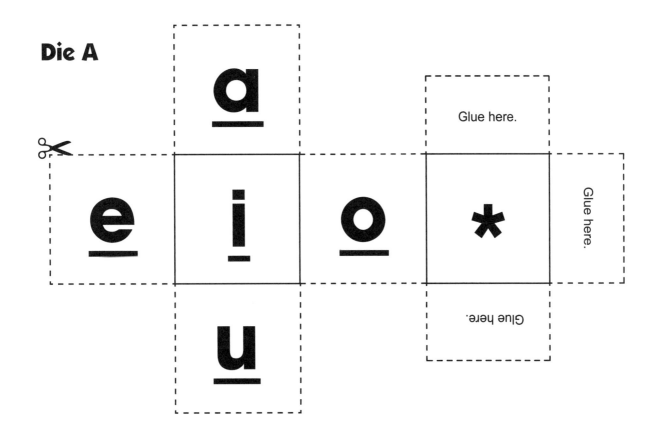

## Die B

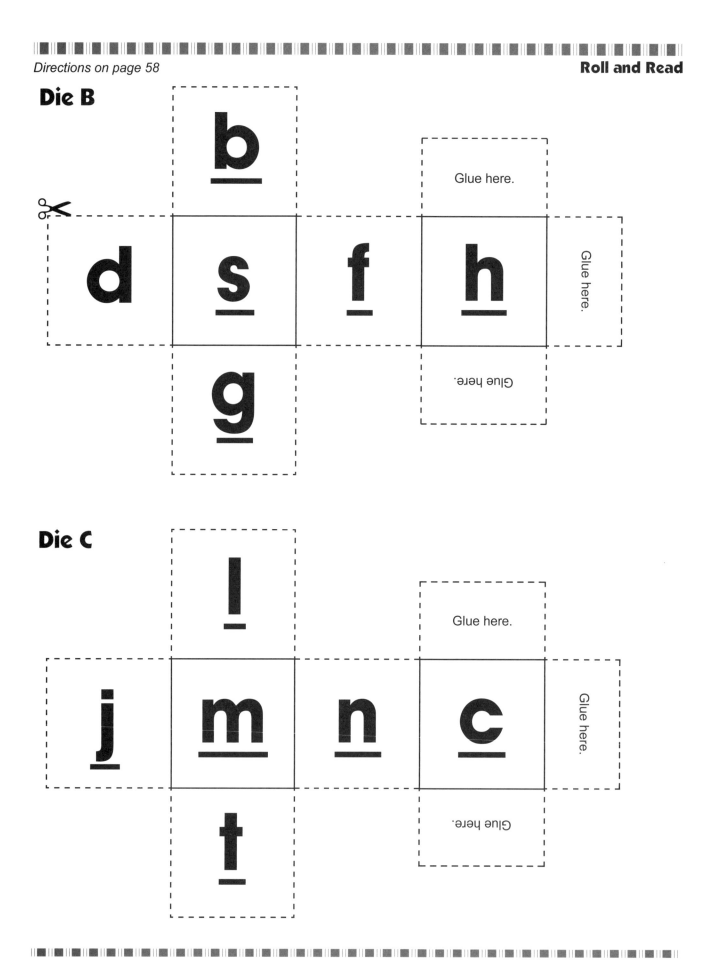

Glue here.

Glue here.

b

d    s    f    h

Glue here.

g

## Die C

l

j    m    n    c

Glue here.

Glue here.

Glue here.

t

# Build a Word

**Getting Ready:** To review some three-letter words, print these two lists of consonants on the board. Then, write the vowels. Print the lists in a similar format as shown below.

| b | b | | | | | |
|---|---|---|---|---|---|---|
| d | d | | | | | |
| h | g | | | | | |
| r | n | a | e | i | o | u |
| s | p | | | | | |
| t | t | | | | | |

**Directions:** Use sentences provided below as word clues. Students must choose an initial consonant from the first list, a final consonant from the second list, and a vowel for the middle of the word to spell each answer.

**Word Clues:**
1. An object that can be seen in the sky during the day is the _____. (sun)
2. An object needed to play baseball is a _____. (bat)
3. Another name for a pig is a _____. (hog)
4. A way of drinking small sips is called _____. (sup)
5. The opposite of *daughter* is _____. (son)
6. The opposite of *cold* is _____. (hot)
7. A female chicken is called a _____. (hen)
8. Shovels are used to _____. (dig)
9. A hamburger is usually eaten on a _____. (bun)
10. Something worn on the head is a _____. (hat)
11. Another name for a sack is a _____. (bag)
12. A bright color is _____. (red)
13. To tear is to _____. (rip)
14. A crying sound is a _____. (sob)
15. An animal that is often a pet is a _____. (dog)
16. A home for a bear is a _____. (den)
17. A short word for father is _____. (dad)
18. An insect is sometimes called a _____. (bug)
19. A number bigger than nine is _____. (ten)
20. An animal that looks like a large mouse is a _____. (rat)

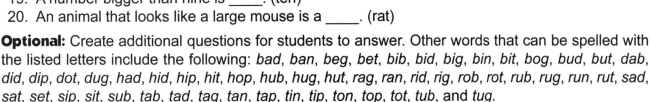

**Optional:** Create additional questions for students to answer. Other words that can be spelled with the listed letters include the following: *bad, ban, beg, bet, bib, bid, big, bin, bit, bog, bud, but, dab, did, dip, dot, dug, had, hid, hip, hit, hop, hub, hug, hut, rag, ran, rid, rig, rob, rot, rub, rug, run, rut, sad, sat, set, sip, sit, sub, tab, tad, tag, tan, tap, tin, tip, ton, top, tot, tub,* and *tug.*

# Slip 'n' Spell Animals

**Getting Ready:** Copy the animals and letter strips on pages 64–68 onto colorful card stock for each student. Also, copy pages 69–71 onto card stock for each group of children. Then, write the missing vowels in the blanks and cut out the cards. Set aside the pictures for the words *nap*, *net*, *zip*, *pot*, and *gum* that cannot be spelled with the Slip 'n' Spell Animals.

**Directions:**

1. Have students decorate their own sets of animals. Then, have them cut out the animals and letter strips.
2. Help children cut the four slits on each animal into which the letter strips will slide. Make sure they put any letter strip ending with two stars in the final consonant position.
3. To practice using the Slip 'n' Spell Animals, say a word from the list on page 63 and have students slide the strips to create the word. Continue in this manner as time and interest allow.

**How to Play:** Use the picture cards on pages 69–71 as the word cards and arrange them facedown in a stack. Have students form groups of two or three players. The first player takes a turn drawing and reading a word for the second player to make on a Slip 'n' Spell Animal. If the second player spells the word correctly, she collects the word card. That player now draws a card for the third player. Continue in this manner for a predetermined length of time.

# Hoppin' on Vowels

**Getting Ready:** Make one copy of the game board and two copies of the game cards on pages 69–73 on colorful card stock for each group of two or three children. Cut out one set of the cards along the dashed lines. Using watercolor markers, decorate the game-board pages as desired. Be sure to highlight the path for students. Trim one of the inside edges of the pages before overlapping them to finish the scene. Then, glue the game-board pages to the inside panels of a file folder. To make the answer key, copy pages 69–71 and then write the missing vowel in each blank. Store the answer sheets along with the game cards and game board in a large envelope. Also, provide a small game marker for each player.

**How to Play:**

1. Shuffle the cards and place them facedown in a stack near the game board.
2. Each player puts a game marker in the GO space.
3. Players take turns drawing a card and turning it faceup. If the player correctly "reads" the word and identifies the missing vowel, he can then move his game marker ahead to the nearest space with that letter on it. The other players must agree that the answer is correct and can check the answer key if needed.
4. The game continues until one player has landed on STOP and is declared the winner.

# Word List for Slip 'n' Spell Animals

| Short A | | Short E | Short I | | Short O | Short U |
|---------|---------|---------|---------|---------|---------|---------|
| bad | jab | bed | bib | lid | cob | bud |
| bag | jam | beg | bid | lip | cod | bug |
| ban | man | bet | big | mix | cot | bus |
| bat | map | den | bin | pig | dog | cub |
| cab | mat | fed | bit | pin | dot | cut |
| can | pan | hen | did | pit | fog | dug |
| cap | pat | jet | dig | rib | fox | fun |
| cat | rag | let | dim | rid | got | hug |
| dab | ram | men | dip | rim | hog | hum |
| dad | ran | met | fib | rip | hop | hut |
| fan | rap | peg | fig | sip | hot | jug |
| fat | rat | pen | fin | sit | jot | mud |
| gab | sad | pet | fit | six | log | mug |
| gag | sag | red | fix | tin | mop | nut |
| gap | sap | set | hid | tip | nod | pup |
| gas | sat | ten | him | wig | not | rug |
| had | tab | vet | hip | win | rob | run |
| ham | tag | | hit | | rod | sub |
| has | tap | | kid | | rot | sun |
| hat | tan | | kin | | sob | tub |
| | | | kit | | | tug |

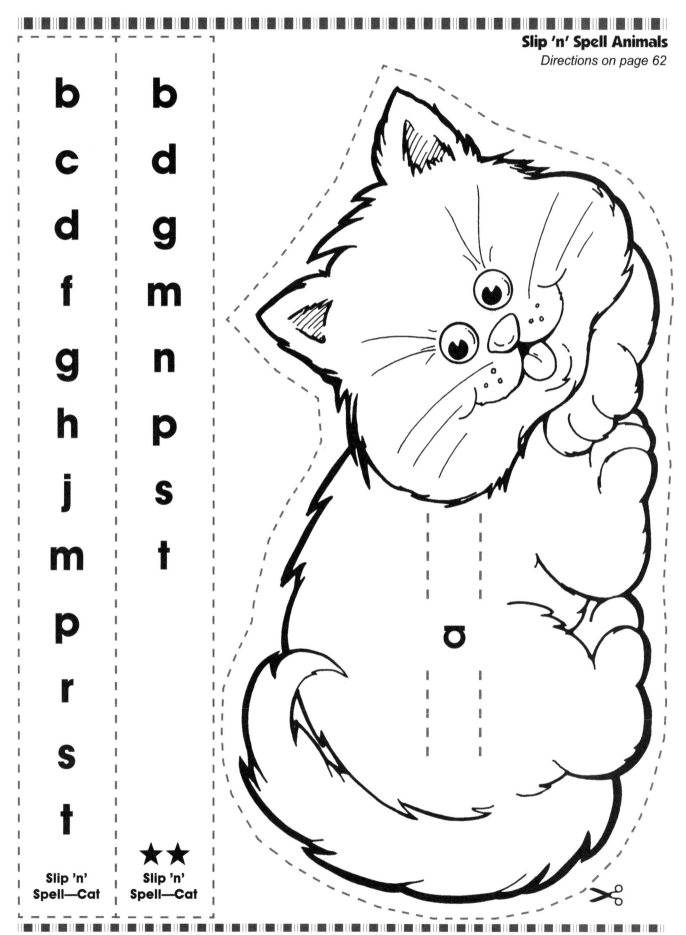

b c d f g h j m p r s t

Slip 'n'
Spell—Cat

b d g m n p s t

★★
Slip 'n'
Spell—Cat

a

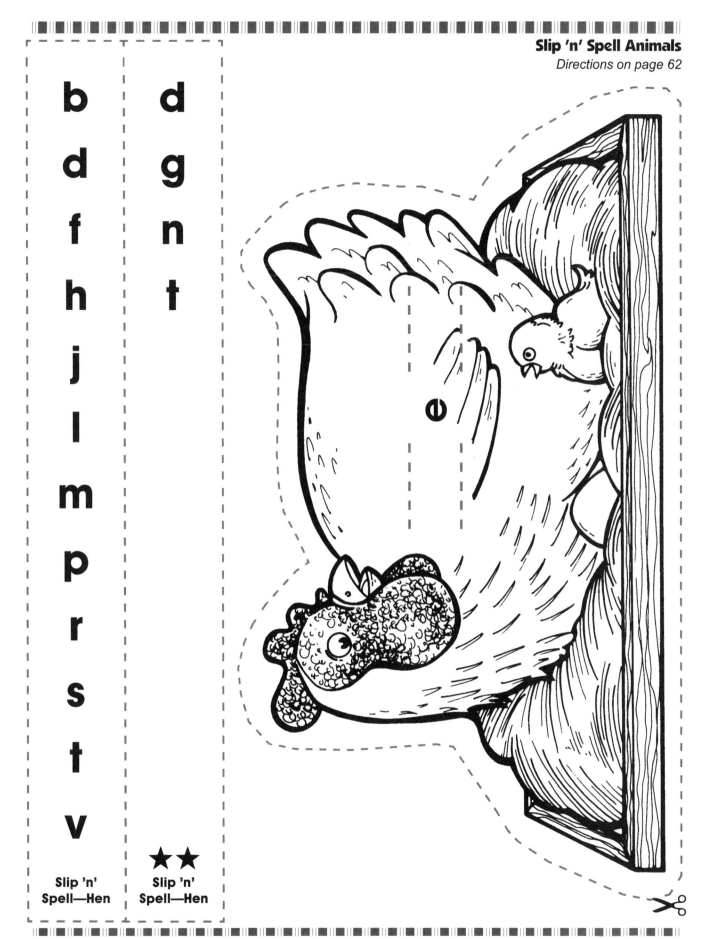

b
d
f
h
j
l
m
p
r
s
t
v

**Slip 'n'
Spell—Hen**

d
g
n
t

★★
**Slip 'n'
Spell—Hen**

b
d
f
h
k
l
m
p
r
s
t
w

**Slip 'n' Spell—Pig**

b
d
g
m
n
p
t
x

★★
**Slip 'n' Spell—Pig**

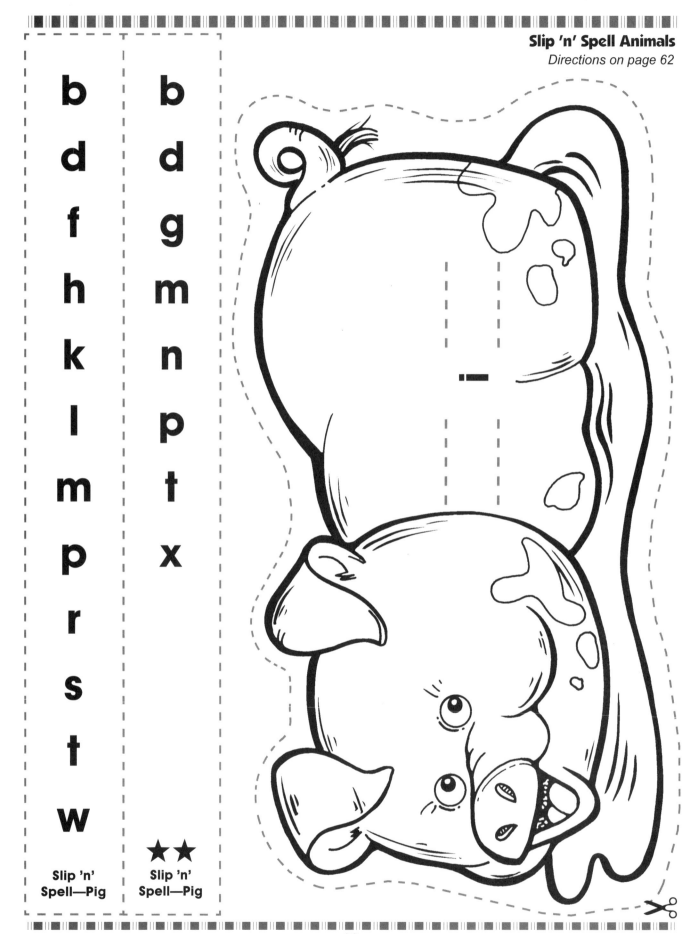

c
d
f
g
h
j
l
m
n
r
s
t

b
d
g
p
t
x

**Slip 'n'
Spell—Fox**

★ ★
**Slip 'n'
Spell—Fox**

b
c
d
f
h
j
m
n
p
r
s
t

**Slip 'n'
Spell—Cub**

b
d
g
p
m
n
s
t

★★
**Slip 'n'
Spell—Cub**

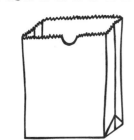

b __ g

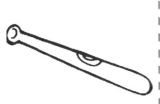

b __ t

c __ b

c __ n

c __ t

f __ n

h __ t

n __ p

r __ t

t __ g

b __ d

j __ t

h __ n

l __ g

m __ n

n __ t

p__n

r__d

t__n

v__t

b__b

f__n

h__t

l__p

p__g

p__n

p__t

w__g

z__p

c__b

c__t

d__g

f __ x

l __ g

m __ p

p __ t

s __ b

t __ p

b __ g

b __ n

b __ s

c __ b

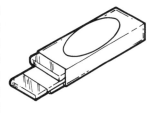

g __ m

j __ g

m __ d

n __ t

s __ b

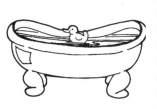

t __ b

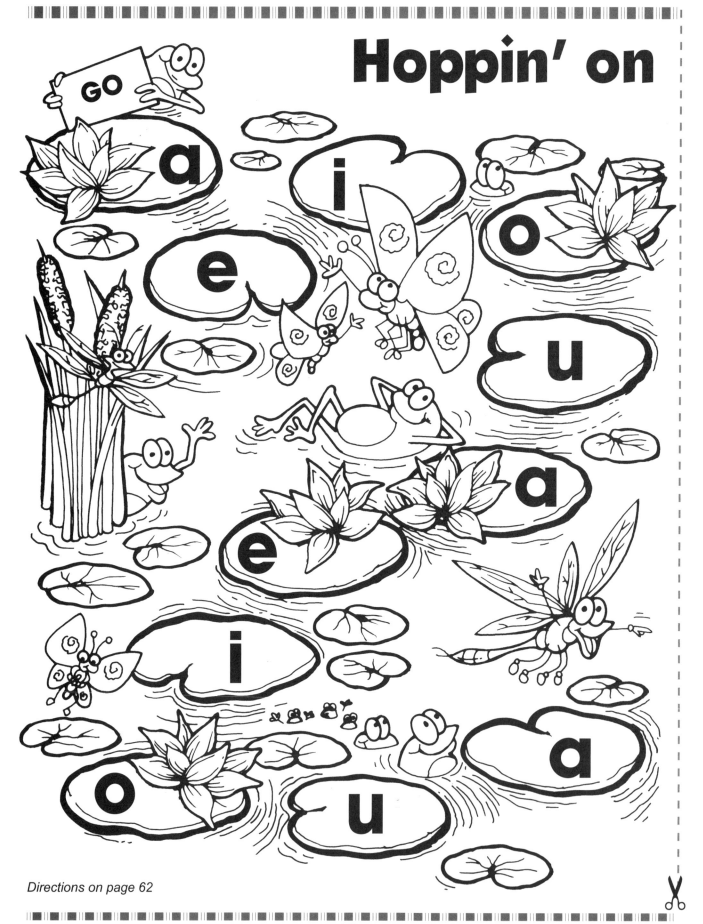

*Directions on page 62*

# Vowels

# Word Sort: A Fun Run!

**Getting Ready:** Copy the word cards on page 75 onto colorful card stock for each pair of students.

**Directions:**
1. Students are to cut out the cards along the dashed lines and then practice reading the words aloud with their partners.
2. Have students sort the set of words two different ways. For example, three groups of words can be formed by using the short-vowel sounds as the categories or two groups of words can be formed by using the final consonant as the category (words ending with the letter *n* and words ending with *t*).

# Bingo Game: A Fun Run!

**Getting Ready:** Copy the bingo boards on pages 76–78 onto colorful card stock for each group of six students. Cut apart the boards along the dashed lines. To prepare the calling cards, copy page 75 onto card stock for each group and cut out the word cards. Give each student nine markers to place on the bingo board.

**How to Play:** Shuffle the word cards. Choose someone to be the "caller." One at a time, the caller announces the word. Each time a student hears a word that is shown on his board, he covers that space with a marker. The first player to cover all squares on her board calls out "I had a fun run!" and is declared the winner.

| | | | | | |
|---|---|---|---|---|---|
| van | rat | win | pit | sun | rut |
| ran | pat | tin | lit | run | nut |
| pan | mat | pin | kit | fun | hut |
| man | hat | fin | hit | bun | gut |
| fan | fat | bin | fit | wit | cut |
| can | cat | sat | bit | sit | but |

# A Fun Run!

Bingo Board #2

| | | |
|---|---|---|
| hat | bin | fan |
| rut | hit | bun |
| pin | cat | fit |

---

# A Fun Run!

Bingo Board #1

| | | |
|---|---|---|
| wit | bun | can |
| ran | hat | tin |
| bit | nut | fun |

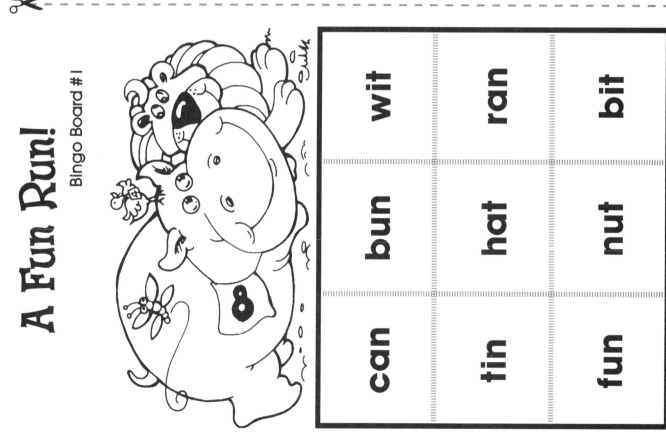

# A Fun Run!
## Bingo Board #4

| mat | rut | pan |
|-----|-----|-----|
| van | lit | sun |
| hut | fin | kit |

# A Fun Run!
## Bingo Board #3

| run | gut | man |
|-----|-----|-----|
| fan | bin | bit |
| pat | lit | sun |

# A Fun Run!

Bingo Board #6

| sit | van | rat |
| --- | --- | --- |
| pin | cut | tin |
| but | fun | mat |

# A Fun Run!

Bingo Board #5

| win | cut | ran |
| --- | --- | --- |
| fun | sat | fin |
| fat | run | pit |

# Build-a-Word Memory Match

**Getting Ready:** For each deck of letter cards, make one copy of page 80 and four copies of page 81 on colorful card stock. (*You may prefer to enlarge the letter cards before photocopying them.*) Cut out the cards along the dashed lines. Set aside seven copies of the letter *y* and three copies of the letters *a, e, i, o, u, and y.* Each deck of cards should include the following letters:

>    One of each—*f, j, v, w, x, y,* and *z*
>    Two of each—*c, g, h, k, l, m,* and *p*
>    Four of each—*b, d, n, r, s,* and *t*
>    Five of each—*a, e, i, o,* and *u*

**How to Play:**

1.  Shuffle the cards and place them facedown in ten rows of seven cards.
2.  Have two or three players take turns flipping over three cards. If the letters on the cards can be used to spell a word, the player says the word and keeps the three cards. If the letters cannot be used, the cards are placed facedown again.
3.  The game continues until one player collects cards for six words and is declared the winner.

# Short-Vowel Rummy

**Getting Ready:** For each deck of cards, make one copy of page 80 and four copies of page 81 on colorful card stock. (*You may prefer to enlarge the letter cards before photocopying them.*) Cut out the cards along the dashed lines. Provide copies of the word families on pages 42 and 43 for children to use as a reference (if needed) when checking the words spelled with the rummy cards.

**How to Play:**

1.  Shuffle the cards.
2.  Deal six cards to each player. Place the remaining cards facedown in a stack.
3.  Have players take turns drawing and discarding a card until one player spells two three-letter (CVC) words and is declared the winner.

| f | j | v | w | z |
|---|---|---|---|---|
| c | g | h | k | l |
| m | p | c | g | h |
| k | l | m | p | x |

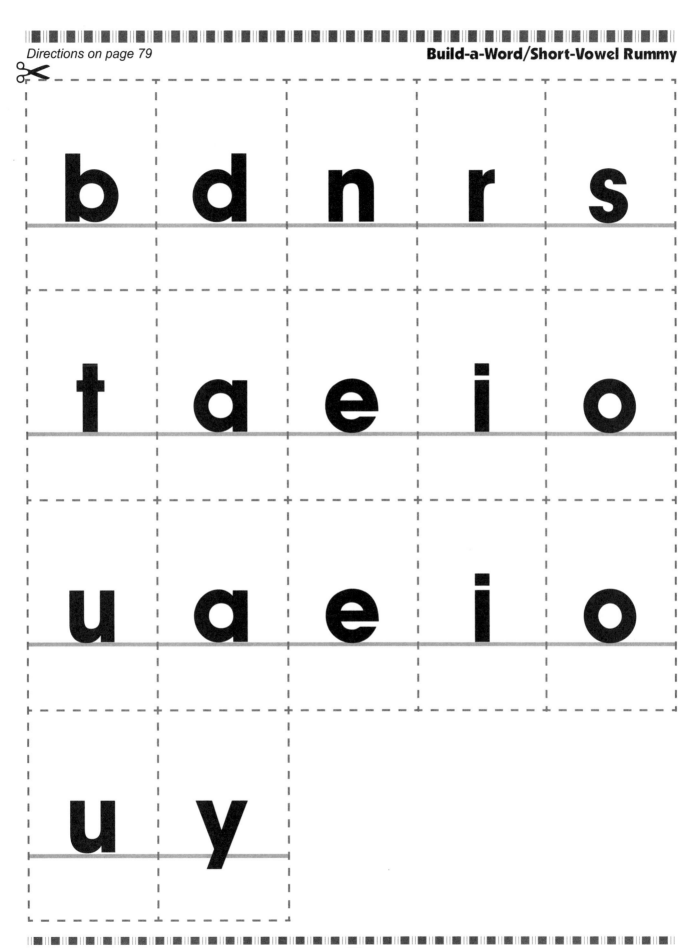

# Phonograms with Blends and Digraphs (CCVC Words)

## Short "a" Families

| -ab | -ad | -am | -an | -ap | -at |
|-----|-----|-----|-----|-----|-----|
| blab* | glad* | clam* | bran* | chap* | chat* |
| crab* | | slam* | clan* | clap | flat* |
| drab* | **-ag** | swam* | plan* | flap | slat* |
| grab* | brag* | tram* | span* | slap* | spat* |
| scab* | flag* | | than* | snap* | that* |
| slab* | | | | trap* | |

*Note:* Due to differences in dialects, certain word families, such as the *-og* family, may not have short-vowel sounds when spoken in your area.

## Short "e" Families

| -ed | -en |
|-----|-----|
| fled* | then* |
| shed | |
| sled* | **-ep** |
| | step* |
| **-em** | |
| stem* | |
| them* | |

## Short "i" Families

| -ib | -ig | -in | -ip | -it |
|-----|-----|-----|-----|-----|
| crib* | twig* | chin* | chip* | slit* |
| | | grin* | drip* | spit* |
| **-id** | **-im** | shin* | flip* | |
| grid* | brim* | skin* | ship* | |
| skid* | slim* | spin* | skip* | |
| slid* | swim* | thin* | slip* | |
| | trim* | twin* | snip* | |
| | | | trip* | |

## Short "o" Families

| -ob | -op | -ot |
|-----|-----|-----|
| blob* | chop | blot* |
| glob* | drop* | shot* |
| snob* | flop* | slot* |
| | plop* | spot* |
| **-og** | prop* | trot |
| clog* | shop* | |
| frog* | stop* | |

## Short "u" Families

| -ub | -ug | -um | -us |
|-----|-----|-----|-----|
| club* | chug* | chum* | plus |
| flub* | drug* | drum* | |
| grub* | plug* | plum* | **-ut** |
| snub* | slug* | swum* | shut* |
| stub* | smug* | | |
| | snug* | | |

*The word is already printed on a card (see pages 89–93).

# Ship Out with Words

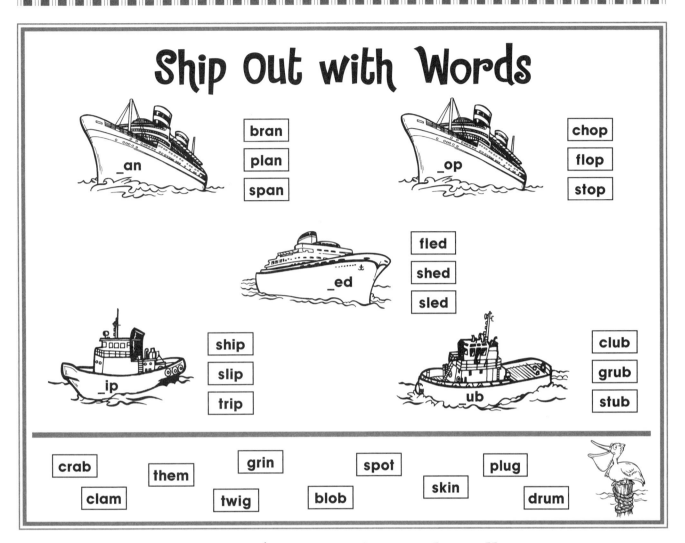

## Bulletin-Board Word Wall

**Getting Ready:** You will need colorful butcher paper, colorful card stock, markers, scissors, stapler, and patterns on pages 85–87 and 89–93.

### Directions:

1. Begin by covering the bulletin board with paper. Arrange the paper so that the top of this display can be reached by standing children if you would like them to point to objects.
2. Copy the title and decorative art on pages 85 and 86 onto colorful card stock. You may prefer to enlarge certain pieces of art before making the reproductions. (Copy the title at 125% to make the lowercase letters about 3 in. [8 cm] in height.) Color the art as desired with markers and then cut out the individual pieces along the dashed lines. Staple the title in the center of the top of the board.
3. Select the phonograms you will introduce and then copy the needed number of ships and tugboats on page 87 onto colorful card stock for displaying the word families. Also, copy and cut out a set of the word cards on pages 89–93.
4. Use a marker to draw a line to create a smaller space below the ship display.
5. Place all materials on a table by the board and then add pieces to the display as new words are introduced during classroom activities. Extra words may be stapled to the bottom of the board.

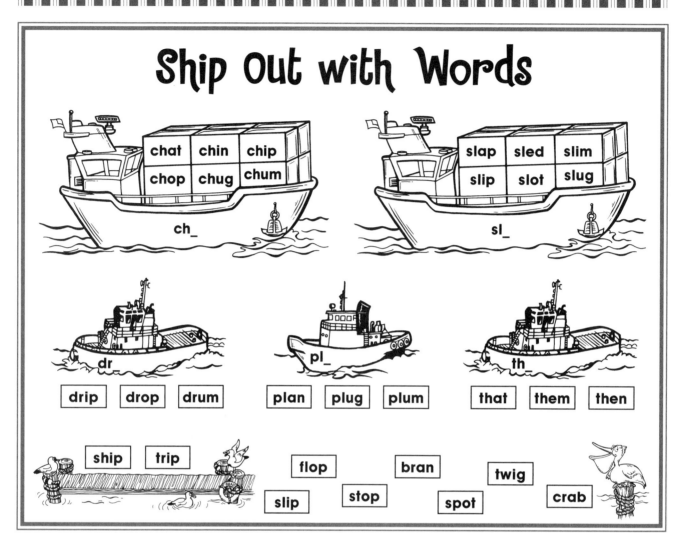

# Bulletin Board for Initial Blends and Digraphs

**Getting Ready:** You will need colorful butcher paper, colorful card stock, markers, scissors, stapler, and patterns on pages 85–93.

**Directions:**

1. Begin by covering the bulletin board with paper. Arrange the paper so that the top of this display can be reached by standing children if you would like them to point to words.

2. Copy the title and decorative art on pages 85 and 86 onto colorful card stock. You may prefer to enlarge certain pieces of art before making the reproductions. (Copy the title at 125% to make the lowercase letters about 3 in. [8 cm] in height.) Color the art as desired with markers and then cut out the individual pieces along the dashed lines. Staple the title in the center of the top of the board.

3. Determine which initial blends and digraphs you will introduce and then copy the needed number of cargo ships and tugboats on pages 87 and 88 onto colorful card stock. Also, copy and cut out a set of the word cards on pages 89–93. (Copy the cargo ship at 150% and the word cards at 85% if you would like to display the words on the art.)

4. Place all materials on a table by the board and then add pieces to the display as new words are introduced during classroom activities. Extra words may be stapled to the bottom of the board.

Spider

With Words

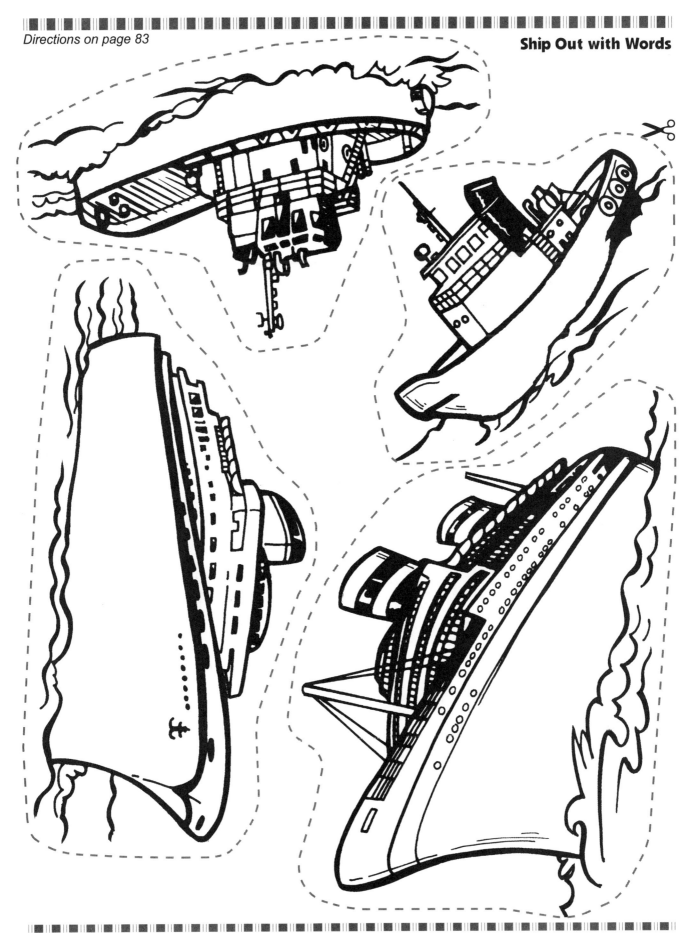

| blab | crab | drab |
| --- | --- | --- |
| grab | scab | slab |
| glad | brag | flag |
| clam | slam | swam |
| tram | bran | clan |
| plan | span | than |

| chap | slap | snap |
|------|------|------|
| trap | chat | flat |
| slat | spat | that |
| fled | sled | stem |
| them | then | step |
| crib | grid | skid |

| slid | twig | brim |
| --- | --- | --- |
| slim | swim | trim |
| chin | grin | shin |
| skin | spin | thin |
| twin | chip | drip |
| flip | ship | skip |

| slip | snip | trip |
|------|------|------|
| slit | spit | blob |
| glob | snob | clog |
| frog | drop | flop |
| plop | prop | shop |
| stop | blot | shot |

| slot | spot | club |
|------|------|------|
| flub | grub | snub |
| stub | chug | drug |
| plug | slug | smug |
| snug | chum | drum |
| plum | swum | shut |

# Word List for Initial Blends and Digraphs

☐ blab*
☐ blob*
☐ blot*
☐ brag*
☐ bran*
☐ brim*
☐ chap*
☐ chat*
☐ chin*
☐ chip*
☐ chop
☐ chug*
☐ chum*
☐ clam*
☐ clan*
☐ clap
☐ clog*
☐ club*
☐ crab*
☐ crib*
☐ drab*
☐ drip*
☐ drop*

☐ drug*
☐ drum*
☐ flag*
☐ flap
☐ flat*
☐ fled*
☐ flip*
☐ flop*
☐ flub*
☐ frog*
☐ glad*
☐ glob*
☐ grab*
☐ grid*
☐ grin*
☐ grub*
☐ plan*
☐ plop*
☐ plug*
☐ plum*
☐ plus
☐ prop*
☐ scab*

☐ shed
☐ shin*
☐ ship*
☐ shop*
☐ shot*
☐ shut*
☐ skid*
☐ skin*
☐ skip*
☐ slab*
☐ slam*
☐ slap*
☐ slat*
☐ sled*
☐ slid*
☐ slim*
☐ slip*
☐ slit*
☐ slot*
☐ slug*
☐ smug*
☐ snap*

☐ snip*
☐ snob*
☐ snub*
☐ snug*
☐ span*
☐ spat*
☐ spin*
☐ spit*
☐ spot*
☐ stem*
☐ step*
☐ stop*
☐ stub*
☐ swam*

☐ swim*
☐ swum*
☐ than*
☐ that*
☐ them*
☐ then*
☐ thin*
☐ tram*
☐ trap*
☐ trim*
☐ trip*
☐ trot
☐ twig*
☐ twin*

*The word is already printed on a card (see pages 89–93).

# Hey, Bliddle Bliddle

**Getting Ready:** On the board, print the following blends: *bl, br, cl, cr, dr, fl, fr, gl, gr, pl, pr, sk, sl, sm, sn, sp, st, sw, tr,* and *tw.* Also, print the nursery rhyme, "Hey, Diddle Diddle," underlining certain words as illustrated below.

> Hey, **diddle diddle**,
> The **cat** and the **fiddle**,
> The **cow** jumped over the **moon**.
> The little **dog** laughed to see such **sport**,
> And the **dish** ran away with the **spoon**.

**Directions:**
1. Make sure everyone knows the nursery rhyme.
2. Have fun replacing the original initial consonants or blends with a different blend to make nonsense words. Say the new rhymes. The following rhyme is the example for *BL.*
   > Hey, **bliddle bliddle**,
   > The **blat** and the **bliddle**,
   > The **blow** jumped over the **bloon**.
   > The little **blog** laughed to see such **blort**,
   > And the **blish** ran away with the **bloon**.
3. Assign each student a blend. Allow time for students to use their assigned blends by printing the rhyme with the new nonsense words and saying it to a partner.
4. In a large group, have children take turns performing the rhymes while others try to identify the blends that were used to make new "words."

# Beginning Sounds Matchups

**Getting Ready:** For each group of two players, copy the game cards on pages 96–102 onto colorful card stock. Cut out the picture and consonant cluster cards along the dashed lines.

**How to Play:** For Level 1, have players set aside the consonant cluster cards and then scatter the picture cards faceup in the center of the playing area. The first player selects three cards and says the names of the pictures. If the three pictures begin with the same sound, the player keeps the cards. If not, the cards are returned to the playing area. The second player now looks for three matching cards. The game continues in this manner until all matching triplets have been found. For Level 2, all cards are used. The players take turns selecting a consonant cluster card and then looking for the corresponding pictures whose names begin with the specified sound. The activity continues until all sets of matching cards are found.

**Optional Play:** Invite students to play a Memory Match game by selecting either pairs of pictures or consonant cluster and picture cards. (Set aside the extra cards.) Arrange the cards facedown in the playing area. The first player selects two cards and turns them faceup. If a match has been found, the player keeps the cards and turns over two more cards. If no match is found, the cards are returned facedown to the playing area. The second player takes a turn. Continue in this manner until all matching cards have been found.

# Beginning Sounds Matchups

| bl | br | cl |
|---|---|---|

Pictures: blocks, blouse, blindfold, bride, brace on child's leg, bricks, clock, clothes in closet, cloud

# Beginning Sounds Matchups

| cr | fl | fr |
|----|----|----|

Pictures: crawl (what the baby does), crib, crown, flamingo, flashlight, fly, frog, frame for a picture, fruit

# Beginning Sounds Matchups

| gl | gr | sl |
|----|----|----|

Pictures: gloves, glue bottle, glasses, grass, grapes, groom, sleigh, slippers, sled

# Beginning Sounds Matchups

| sw | tr | tw |
|----|----|----|

Pictures: sweep, swing (action of girl), swat (trying to swat the fly), tractor, tree, truck, twenty, twins, twelve

# Beginning Sounds Matchups

Pictures: drum, dragon, dress, plate, platypus, plant, pretzels, princess, propeller

# Beginning Sounds Matchups

| sk | sn | st |
|----|----|-----|

Pictures: skates, skunk, skirt, snail, snake, snowman and snowflakes, starfish, stapler, stove

# Beginning Sounds Matchups

| ch | sh | th |
|----|----|----|

Pictures: chess, chair, cherries, shoe, sheep, shark, thumb, thirty, thirteen

# Which Beginning Sound: SM or SW?

**Getting Ready:** On the board, list the following words: *smug\**, *swim\**, *swam\**, and *swum\**.

**Directions:**

1. Introduce the words by reading them aloud. Stretch the sounds in the words as you move a finger under the letters to demonstrate how to blend the sounds. Then, read the words aloud in a normal manner. Discuss the meanings of the words if necessary.
2. Say each word and have students identify the initial sounds with a hand signal (three middle fingers of one hand held up for the letter *SW* or held down for *SM*).
3. Next, say other *SM* or *SW* words and have students identify the blend with the appropriate number of fingers. Examples include *swallow*, *smile*, *smoke*, *smart*, *sweet*, and *swing*.

**Culmination:** Select the words you would like to add to the "Ship Out with Words" bulletin-board word wall and print them on small index cards that have been cut in half. Label the word families on the appropriate shapes and display them with the words. (*Note:* Words above marked with an asterick are provided on pages 89–93.)

# Which Sound: CL, FL, GL, PL, or SL?

**Getting Ready:** For each group of two to four players, you will need the four dice on pages 105 and 106, scissors, and glue. Copy the dice patterns onto colorful card stock and cut them out along the dashed lines. Fold each pattern along the solid lines to form a cube shape. Glue the tabs as indicated on the dice. Make a copy of the picture cards on page 104 for each pair of students. On the board, list the following words: *clam\**, *clan\**, *clap*, *clog\**, *club\**, *flag\**, *flap*, *flat\**, *fled\**, *flip\**, *flop\**, *flub\**, *glob\**, *plop\**, *plug\**, *plum\**, *slab\**, *slam\**, *slap\**, *sled\**, *slid\**, *slim\**, *slip\**, *slit\**, *slot\**, and *slug\**.

**Directions:**

1. Begin by reading aloud the words, one at a time, listed on the board. Make the initial consonant blend sound while pointing to the letter clusters. Stretch out the sounds of the selected words to demonstrate how to blend the individual phonemes together. Then, read the words aloud again in a normal manner. Discuss the meanings of the words if necessary.
2. Read the words in random order. At times, also say a word that is not written on the board. Ask students to hold up the picture whose name begins with the same blend or point to the correct word on the board. Have students hold up their trash can pictures when there is no match.

**How to Play:** In each group, players take turns rolling all four of the dice. The first player attempts to spell as many words as possible with the letters indicated by the roll by writing them on a sheet of paper. *Note:* The asterisk can be used for any one of the five blends: *cl, fl, gl, pl,* or *sl*. Once a player indicates that an asterisk represents a particular blend, she must use it as that blend in all of the words she spells on that particular turn. At the end of a predetermined time or specified number of rounds, words on the lists are checked and counted. The player with the most words is declared the winner.

**Culmination:** Follow the directions provided in the previous activity for the bulletin-board word wall.

Pictures: clam, flag, gloves, plums, sled, trash can

**Die A**

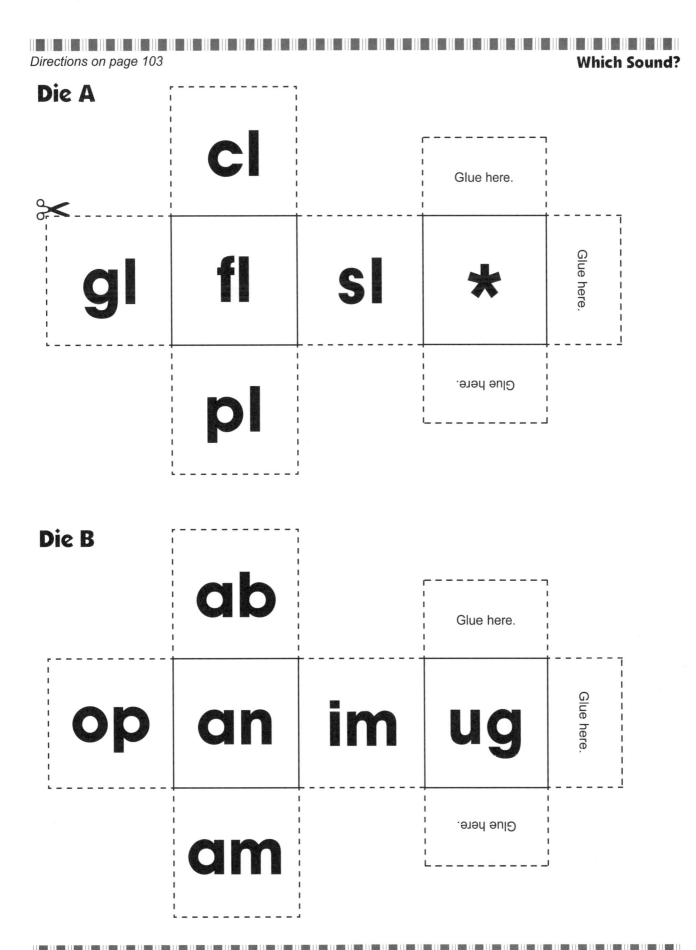

**Die B**

**Die C**

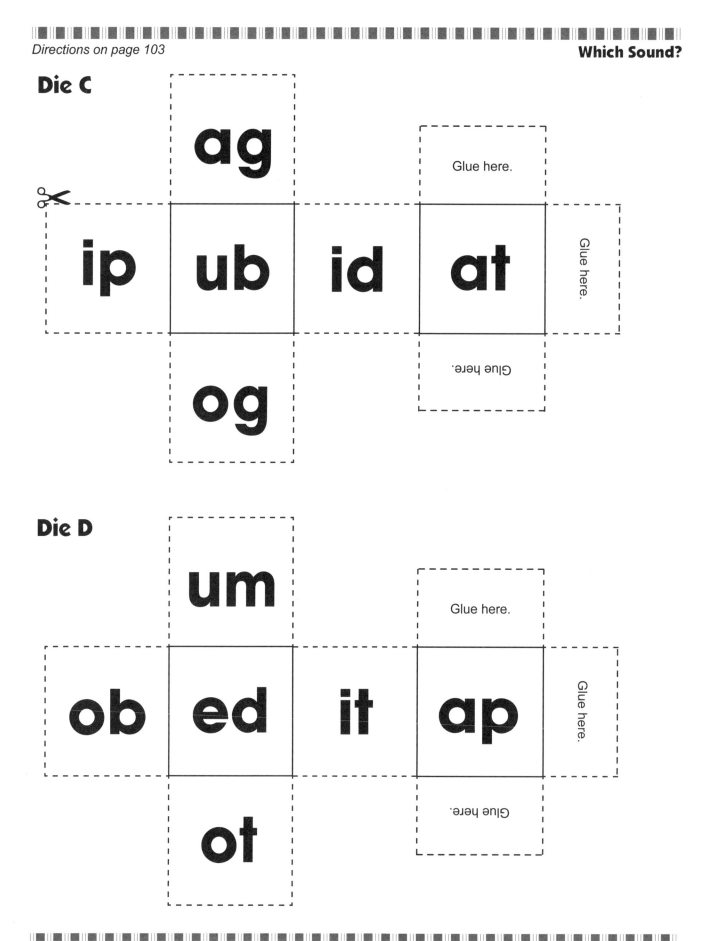

ag

ip ub id at

Glue here.

Glue here.

Glue here.

og

**Die D**

um

ob ed it ap

Glue here.

Glue here.

Glue here.

ot

# Which Sound: *BL* or *BR*?

**Getting Ready:** On the board, print the following words in random order: *blab\**, *blip*, *blob\**, *blot\**, *brag\**, *bran\**, *brat*, and *brim\**.

**Directions:**

1. Choose a word and then read it aloud by stretching the sounds in the word. Move a finger under each letter as its phoneme is spoken. Repeat this step several times to help children distinguish the sounds of the blends /bl/ and /br/.
2. Randomly read aloud each word displayed on the board. Have students take turns pointing to the words.
3. Ask students to print pairs of words on their paper as you dictate them. They may refer to the list on the board for spelling the words.
   Examples:
   1. blot, brag     2. brim, blab     3. blob, brat     4. blip, blot     5. bran, brag

**Culmination:** Select the words you would like to add to the "Ship Out with Words" bulletin-board word wall and print them on small index cards that have been cut in half. Label the word families on the appropriate shapes and display them with the words. (*Note*: Words above marked with an asterisk are provided on pages 89–93.)

# Word Turners

**Getting Ready:** Have students print the letters *s* and *t* individually on index cards.

**Directions:** Write the word *pan* on the board. Ask, "Which letter turns *pan* into *span*?" Have students look at their letter cards and hold up the letter that best completes the word. Choose one student to come forward and print the letter *s* in front of the word *pan*. Practice the steps again with one of the following questions.

Which letter turns *pot* into *spot\**?          Which letter turns *win* into *twin\**?
Which letter turns *rip* into *trip\**?          Which letter turns *nip* into *snip\**?
Which letter turns *nap* into *snap\**?          Which letter turns *tub* into *stub\**?
Which letter turns *wig* into *twig\**?          Which letter turns *wig* into *twig\**?
Which letter turns *pat* into *spat\**?          Which letter turns *kit* into *skit*?
Which letter turns *pin* into *spin\**?          Which letter turns *rim* into *trim\**?
Which letter turns *cat* into *scat*?          Which letter turns *cab* into *scab\**?
Which letter turns *rap* into *trap\**?          Which letter turns *rot* into *trot*?

**How to Play:** Have the students form groups of six players and use only one card for *s* and one card for *t*. Read a question from the list above and write the specified word on the board. Each team looks for the letter that best completes the new word and sends the letter card with its walker to the front of the class. If the letter choice is correct, that team earns a point. The walkers return to the teams with their letter cards. Continue playing until eight questions have been asked. There may be one or more winning teams.

**Culmination:** Follow the directions provided in the previous activity for the bulletin-board word wall.

# Slip 'n' Spell Crab

**Getting Ready:** Copy the Slip 'n' Spell Crab and letter strips on page 109 onto colorful card stock for each student. Make one copy of the word cards on page 110 onto card stock for each group of players and then cut apart the cards along the dashed lines.

**Directions:**

1. Students are to decorate and cut out their own Slip 'n' Spell Crabs. They can also cut out the paper strips.
2. Help students cut the four slits on their crabs into which the letter strips will slide. Make sure they put the strip with two stars showing the word families in the final position.
3. Say words from the list below and have students slide the strips to create the words accordingly. Continue in this manner as time and interest allow.

**How to Play:** Have students form groups of two or three players. Arrange the word cards facedown in a stack. Have students take turns drawing and reading words for another player to make on a Slip 'n' Spell Crab. Each time a player spells a word correctly, that player collects the word card. Continue playing the game in this manner for a predetermined length of time.

✂ - - - - - - - - - - - - - - - - - - - - - - - - - - - - - - - - - - -

# Slip 'n' Spell Word List

| | | | | |
|---|---|---|---|---|
| ☐ cab | ☐ tan | ☐ cop | ☐ brag | ☐ grab |
| ☐ dab | ☐ bid | ☐ top | ☐ bran | ☐ grid |
| ☐ gab | ☐ did | ☐ cub | ☐ brim | ☐ grin |
| ☐ tab | ☐ dim | ☐ dub | ☐ crab | ☐ grip |
| ☐ bag | ☐ bin | ☐ tub | ☐ crop | ☐ grub |
| ☐ gag | ☐ tin | ☐ bug | ☐ drab | ☐ trim |
| ☐ tag | ☐ dip | ☐ dug | ☐ drip | ☐ trip |
| ☐ can | ☐ tip | ☐ tug | ☐ drop | |
| | | | ☐ drug | |

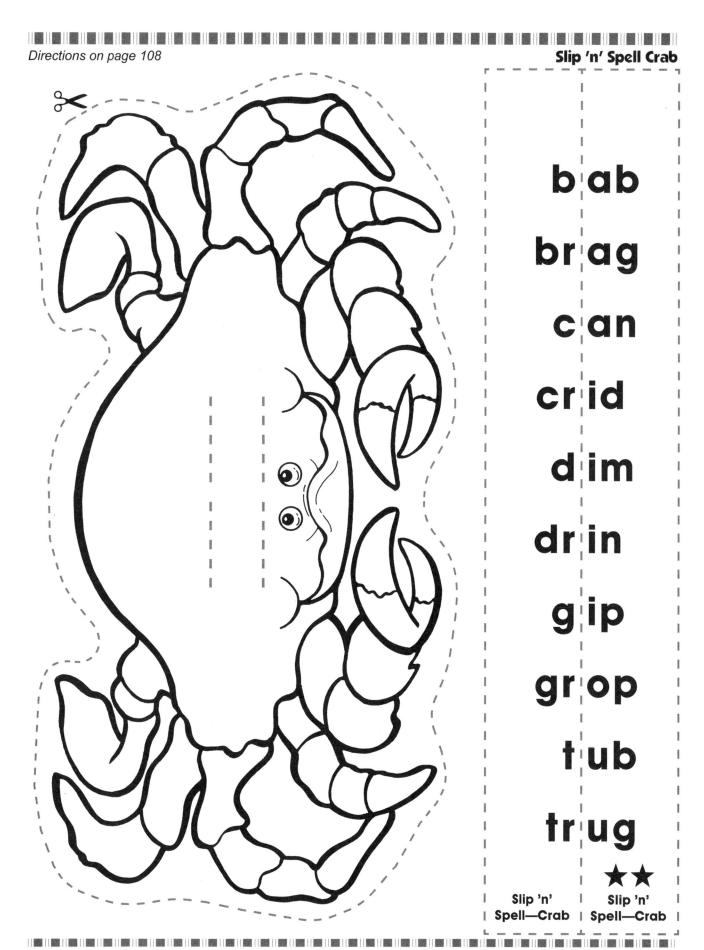

**b ab**

**br ag**

**c an**

**cr id**

**d im**

**dr in**

**g ip**

**gr op**

**t ub**

**tr ug**

★★

Slip 'n'
Spell—Crab

Slip 'n'
Spell—Crab

| | | | | | |
|---|---|---|---|---|---|
| gag | dim | top | tug | drab | grin |
| bag | did | cop | dug | crop | grid |
| tab | bid | tip | bug | crab | grab | trip |
| gab | tan | dip | tub | brim | drug | trim |
| dab | can | tin | dub | bran | drop | grub |
| cab | tag | bin | cub | brag | drip | grip |

# Flip-Flop Bingo

**Getting Ready:** Make copies of the bingo boards on pages 112–114 onto colorful card stock for each group of six students. Cut apart the boards along the dashed lines. To prepare the calling cards, copy page 115 onto card stock for each group and cut out the word cards. Give each student nine markers to place on the bingo board.

**How to Play:** Shuffle the picture cards. Choose someone to be the "caller." One at a time, the caller announces the name of the animal in the picture. When a student hears the blend sound for a letter cluster that is shown on her board, she covers that space with a marker. The first player to cover all squares on his board calls out "Flip-Flop Bingo" and is declared the winner.

# Who Is Holding . . . ?

**Getting Ready:** Copy the word cards on pages 89–93 onto card stock. Cut out the cards along the dashed lines. Select words that are familiar to students.

**How to Play:** For this activity, give each student two or three cards. Have four students each bring one of their word cards to the front of the class and display them for others to see. Give a clue about one of the words. Have a student answer the clue and then identify who is holding the card. For example: Ask, "What is the name for a banner that is displayed on a tall pole?" The first student to answer correctly (e.g., *flag*) chooses a word card and comes to the front of the group to exchange places with the person who held the mystery word (e.g., *flag*).

# Spin for Cargo

**Getting Ready:** Copy the spinner card on page 116 and three copies of the game board on page 117 for each group of three players. Also, make a copy of the word cards on pages 89–93 at 90% reduction onto card stock. Cut out the cards along the dashed lines. Select 30 words for each group of players to decode. Provide a paper clip and pencil for the spinner dial as shown below.

**How to Play:** Shuffle the word cards and place them facedown near the game board. First, determine which player begins the game. Have players take turns spinning the paper clip, drawing the corresponding number of word cards, and reading the words aloud. Each time a word is read correctly, the player can place that card on one of the shipping cartons on her game board. The first player to collect eight cards is declared the winner.

# Flip-Flop Bingo
### Board #2

| bl | sk | st |
| --- | --- | --- |
| sw | cl | tw |
| fl | sn | sl |

# Flip-Flop Bingo
### Board #1

| sk | sp | bl |
| --- | --- | --- |
| sn | sl | sw |
| cl | gl | fl |

# Flip-Flop Bingo
### Board #4

| cl | fl | tw |
|----|----|----|
| pl | sn | bl |
| gl | sl | st |

# Flip-Flop Bingo
### Board #3

| sw | cl | pl |
|----|----|----|
| sl | fl | sk |
| sp | st | tw |

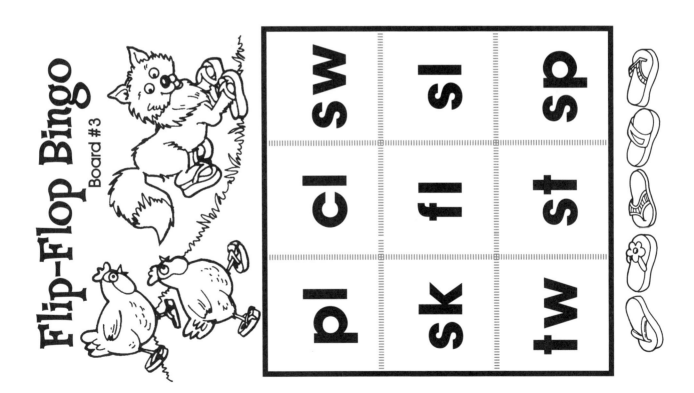

# Flip-Flop Bingo
### Board #6

| fl | bl | sw |
|----|----|----|
| st | pl | cl |
| sn | gl | sp |

# Flip-Flop Bingo
### Board #5

| sn | st | gl |
|----|----|----|
| bl | sp | fl |
| sk | tw | pl |

**114**

Pictures: clock, flashlight, skunk, sled, snake, stapler, swing, blouse, gloves, plant, twins, spider

# Spin for Cargo

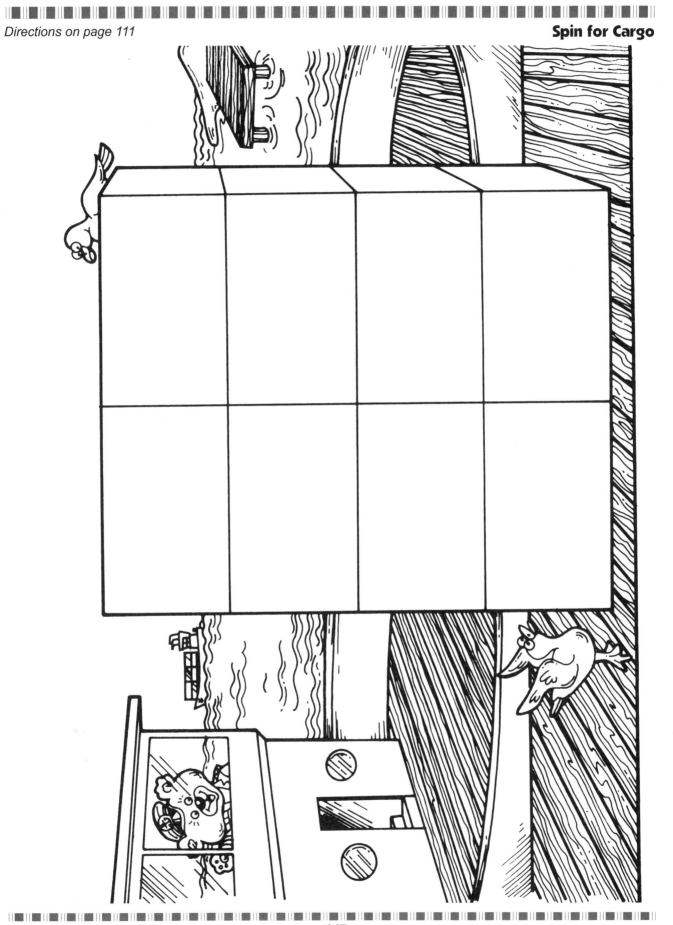

# More Short-Vowel Phonograms
## (CVCC & CCVCC Words)

## Short "a" Families

*Note*: Due to differences in dialects, certain word families may not have short-vowel sounds when spoken in your area.

| -ack | -amp | -ang | -ank | -ash | -ass | -ath |
|------|------|------|------|------|------|------|
| back* | camp | bang* | bank | cash* | bass | bath |
| black | champ* | clang | blank* | clash | brass | math |
| crack | clamp | fang | clank | dash | class* | path |
| jack* | cramp | gang | crank | flash | glass* | |
| lack | damp | hang | drank | gash | pass* | |
| pack* | lamp* | pang | flank | mash | | |
| rack | stamp* | rang* | plank | rash | | |
| sack | | sang* | rank | sash | **-ast** | |
| shack | **-and** | slang | sank* | slash | blast* | |
| smack | band* | | tank* | smash* | cast | |
| snack* | bland | | thank* | trash* | fast* | |
| tack | hand* | | yank | | last | |
| track | land | | | | mast | |
| | sand* | | | | past* | |
| | stand | | | | | |

## Short "e" Families

| -eck | -ell | -end | -ent | -ept | -ess | -est |
|------|------|------|------|------|------|------|
| check* | bell* | bend* | bent | crept* | bless | best* |
| deck* | dwell | blend | cent | kept* | chess* | blest |
| fleck | fell* | end | dent | slept | dress* | chest* |
| neck* | sell* | lend | lent | swept | less | crest |
| speck | shell | mend | rent* | | mess* | nest |
| peck | smell | send* | sent | | press | pest |
| | spell* | spend* | spent* | | | quest |
| **-elf** | swell | tend | tent* | | | rest |
| elf | tell | | went | | | test* |
| self | well | | | | | vest* |
| shelf | yell | | | | | west |
| | | | | | | zest |

*The word is already printed on a card. (See pages 126–131.)*

## Short "i" Families

| -ick | -ift | -ill | -imp | -ing | -ink | -int | -iss |
|------|------|------|------|------|------|------|------|
| brick* | drift | bill* | blimp | bring* | blink* | hint* | hiss |
| chick* | gift* | chill | chimp* | cling | brink | lint | kiss |
| flick | lift* | dill | limp* | ding | clink | mint* | miss |
| kick* | rift | drill | skimp | fling | drink* | print* | |
| lick | shift | fill* | | king* | link | | |
| pick | sift | gill | | ping | mink | **-ish** | **-ist** |
| quick* | swift | grill | | ring* | pink* | dish* | fist* |
| sick* | | hill* | | sing* | rink | fish* | list* |
| slick | | mill | | sling | shrink | swish | mist |
| stick | | pill | | sting | sink* | wish* | twist* |
| thick | | sill | | swing | stink | | |
| trick | | skill | | thing | wink | | |
| wick | | spill | | wing | | | |
| | | still* | | zing | | | |
| | | will* | | | | | |

## Short "o" Families

| -ock | -oft |
|------|------|
| block* | loft |
| clock* | soft |
| dock | |
| flock | **-omp** |
| lock* | chomp |
| mock | stomp |
| rock* | |
| shock | **-ond** |
| smock | blond |
| sock | bond |
| | fond |
| | pond |

## Short "u" Families

| -uck | -ull | -ump | -unk | -ust |
|------|------|------|------|------|
| buck* | dull | bump | bunk* | crust |
| cluck | gull | clump | chunk | dust* |
| duck* | hull | dump* | junk* | gust |
| luck* | lull | grump | sunk | just |
| puck | skull | jump* | skunk* | must* |
| stuck | | lump | stunk | trust* |
| truck* | | plump* | | |
| tuck | | slump* | **-ush** | |
| | | | brush* | |
| **-uff** | | **-ung** | crush* | |
| bluff* | muff | clung | flush | |
| cuff* | puff | flung* | hush* | |
| gruff* | stuff* | hung | rush* | |
| huff | | rung* | slush | |
| | | stung* | | |
| | | swung | | |

*The word is already printed on a card. (See pages 126–131.)

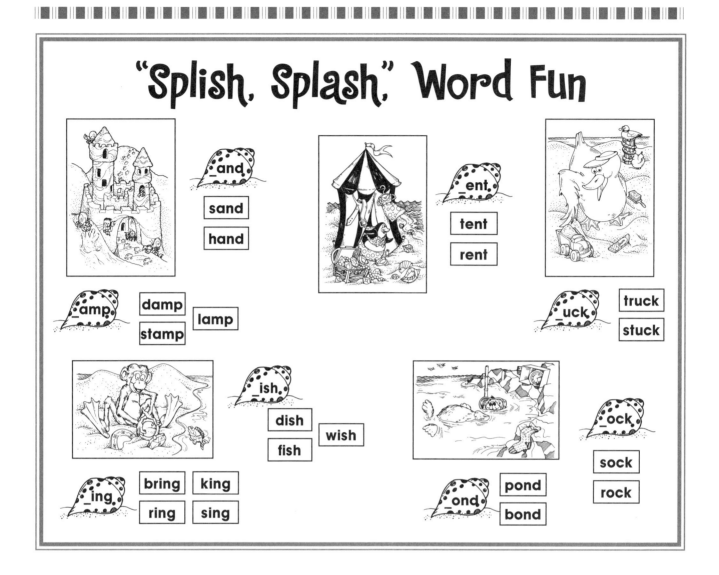

## Bulletin-Board Word Wall

**Getting Ready:** You will need colorful butcher paper, card stock, markers, scissors, stapler, and patterns on pages 121–131.

**Directions:**

1. Begin by covering the bulletin board with paper. Arrange the paper so that the top of this display can be reached by standing children if you would like them to point to words.

2. Copy the title and decorative art on pages 121–125 onto card stock. You may prefer to enlarge the art before making the reproduction. (Copy the title at 125% to make the lowercase letters about 3 in. [8 cm] in height.) Color the art as desired with markers and then cut out the individual pieces along the dashed lines. Staple the title in the center of the top of the board.

3. Select the phonograms you will introduce and then draw seashells on card stock for displaying the word families individually. Copy the word cards on pages 126–131 onto card stock and cut them out.

4. Place all materials on a table by the board and then add the pieces to the display as new words are introduced during classroom activities.

**122**

# Short "e" Sound

# Short "a" Sound

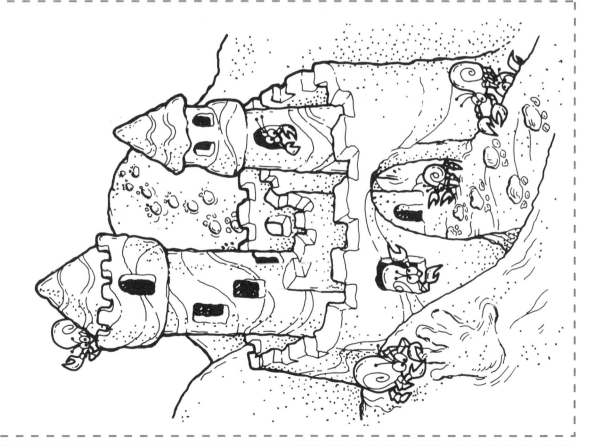

# Short "i" Sound

# Short "o" Sound

# Short "u" Sound

# "Splish, Splash," Word Fun

| back | jack | pack |
| --- | --- | --- |
| snack | champ | lamp |
| stamp | band | hand |
| sand | bang | rang |
| sang | blank | sank |
| tank | thank | cash |

| smash | trash | class |
| --- | --- | --- |
| glass | pass | blast |
| fast | past | check |
| deck | neck | bell |
| fell | sell | spell |
| bend | send | spend |

| rent | spent | tent |
|------|-------|------|
| crept | kept | chess |
| dress | mess | best |
| chest | test | vest |
| brick | chick | kick |
| quick | sick | gift |

| lift | bill | fill |
| hill | still | will |
| chimp | limp | bring |
| king | ring | sing |
| blink | drink | pink |
| sink | hint | mint |

| print | dish | fish |
| wish | fist | list |
| twist | block | clock |
| lock | rock | buck |
| duck | luck | truck |
| bluff | cuff | gruff |

| | | |
|---|---|---|
| **stuff** | **dump** | **jump** |
| **plump** | **slump** | **flung** |
| **rung** | **stung** | **bunk** |
| **junk** | **skunk** | **brush** |
| **crush** | **hush** | **rush** |
| **dust** | **must** | **trust** |

# The Short Vowel Song

**Directions:** Teach students "The Short Vowel Song," sung to the tune of "The Wheels on the Bus Go 'Round and 'Round."

> *Short **a** in a word goes /a/ - /a/ - /a/, (Sing the short a sound as in <u>a</u>pple.)*
> */a/ - /a/ - /a/,*
> */a/ - /a/ - /a/.*
> *Short **a** in a word goes /a/ - /a/ - /a/*
> *In all short **a** words!*

Additional Verses:

*Short **e** in a word goes /e/ - /e/ - /e/, (Sing the short e sound as in b<u>e</u>d.) . . .*
*Short **i** in a word goes /i/ - /i/ - /i/, (Sing the short i sound as in p<u>i</u>g.) . . .*
*Short **o** in a word goes /o/ - /o/ - /o/, (Sing the short o sound as in t<u>o</u>p.) . . .*
*Short **u** in a word goes /u/ - /u/ - /u/, (Sing the short u sound as in s<u>u</u>b.) . . .*

# Rhyming Words Matchups

**Getting Ready:** For each group of two players, copy the game cards on pages 133–139 onto colorful card stock. Cut out the picture and phonogram cards along the dashed lines. Sort the cards into sets and store them in small envelopes that have been labeled.

**How to Play:** For Level 1, have players set aside the phonogram cards and then scatter the picture cards faceup in the center of the playing area. The first player selects two cards and says the names of the pictures. If the pair of cards rhyme, the player keeps the cards. If not, the cards are returned to the playing area. The second player then looks for a matching pair of cards. The game continues in this manner until all pairs of matching cards have been found. For Level 2, the players must also match each pair of pictures with the corresponding phonogram card.

**Optional Play:** Invite students to play a Memory Match game by selecting either pairs of rhyming pictures or phonogram and picture cards. Then, set aside the extra cards. Arrange the cards facedown in the center of the playing area. The first player selects two cards and turns them faceup. If a match has been found, the player keeps the cards and turns over two more cards. If no match is found, the cards are returned facedown to the playing area. The second player then looks for matching cards. The game continues until all pairs of matching cards have been found. The winner is the player who has collected the most cards.

# Rhyming Words Matchups

| | | |
|---|---|---|
| **_amp** | **_ank** | **_ump** |
| **_unk** |  |  |
|  |  |  |
|  |  |  |

Pictures: lamp, stamp, bank, tank (air tank), jump (as an action), pump, bunk (beds), skunk

# Rhyming Words Matchups

| _end | _elf | _ock |
|------|------|------|
| _uck |  |  |
|  |  |  |
|  |  |  |

Pictures: blend (as an action), bend (as an action), shelf, elf, clock, block, duck, truck

**134**

# Rhyming Words Matchups

## _ish

## _ush

## _ash

## _ast

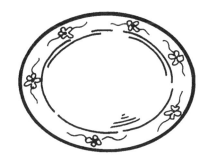

Pictures: dish, fish, brush, slush (melting snow), trash, cash, cast, fast (as an action)

# Rhyming Words Matchups

| **_ack** | **_ick** | **_ing** |
| --- | --- | --- |
| **_imp** |  |  |
| 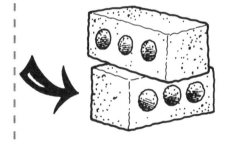 |  |  |
|  |  |  |

Pictures: jack, backpack, brick, chick, ring, king, chimp, blimp

# Rhyming Words Matchups

_ell

_ill

_ull

_ink

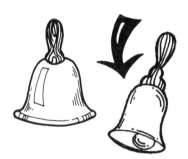

Pictures: shell (seashell), bell, bill, hill, hull, gull (seagull), rink (skating rink), stink (as an action)

# Rhyming Words Matchups

| | | |
|---|---|---|
| **_ent** | **_est** | **_ess** |
| **_ust** |  |  |
|  |  |  |
|  |  | 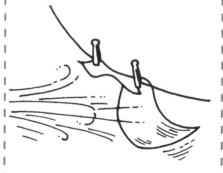 |

Pictures: dent, tent, vest, nest, chess, dress, crust, gust (wind)

# Rhyming Words Matchups

| | | |
|---|---|---|
| **_and** | **_ift** | **_ist** |
| **_uff** | | |

Pictures: band, hand, gift, lift (as an action), list, twist (as an action), huff (as an action), cuff

# Here We Go Rhyming

**Getting Ready:** List the following rhyming words on the board.

*back\*, jack\*, lack, pack\*, rack, sack, tack*
*bang\*, fang, rang\*, sang\**
*bent, cent, dent, rent\*, tent\*, went*
*best\*, nest, pest, rest, test\*, west*
*dish\*, fish\*, wish\**
*kick\*, lick, pick, sick\*, wick*
*king\*, ring\*, sing\*, wing*
*dock, lock\*, rock\*, sock*
*bump, dump\*, jump\*, lump*

**Directions:** Teach students the song "Here We Go Rhyming," sung to the tune of "Here We Go 'Round the Mulberry Bush." Teacher circles the word *best* and sings:

*What is a word that rhymes with **best**,*
*Rhymes with **best**, rhymes with **best**?*
*What is a word that rhymes with **best**?*
*Easy is the rhyming.* (Chooses a student to reply.)

Student calls out the word *test* and everyone sings:

**Test** *is a word that rhymes with **best**,*
*Rhymes with **best**, rhymes with **best**.*
**Test** *is a word that rhymes with **best**.*
*Easy is the rhyming.*

Teacher circles *test* and sings:

*Name another word that rhymes with **test**,*
*Rhymes with **test**, rhymes with **test**.*
*Name another word that rhymes with **test**.*
*Easy is the rhyming.* (Chooses another student to reply.)

**Culmination:** Select the words you would like to add to the "'Splish, Splash,' Word Fun" bulletin-board word wall and print them on small index cards that have been cut in half. Label the word families on the appropriate shapes and include them with the words. (*Note*: Words above marked with an asterisk are provided on pages 126–131.)

# Sing and Spell with Double L

**Getting Ready:** On the board, list the following short vowel words: *bell\**, *bill\**, *dell*, *dill*, *dull*, *fell*, *fill\**, *gill*, *gull*, *hill\**, *hull*, *jell*, *lull*, *mill*, *mull*, *pill*, *sell\**, *sill*, *tell*, *well*, *will\**, and *yell*. Also, print the words on small index cards for the culminating activity.

**Directions:** Teach students "The Double L Song," sung to the chorus of "Jingle Bells."

> *Double L's,*
> *Double L's,*
> *We spell with double L's.*
> *Oh, what fun it is to spell*
> *Words that end with L's.*

For each additional verse, point to a double *L* word on the board, such as the word *bell*. Then, have the students sing the song to spell the chosen word.

> **B-e-l-l, b-e-l-l,**
> **B-e-l-l—bell.**
> *Oh, what fun it is to spell*
> *Words that end with L's.*

Repeat the song with other double *L* words as time and interest allow.

**Culmination:** Place the index cards in your literacy work station and have students work with partners to sort the cards into word families. If other double *L* words are found by students, include those words in the set of cards, too. When students are finished with the activity, add the words to "'Splish, Splash' Word Fun" bulletin-board word wall. (*Note:* Words above marked with an asterisk are provided on pages 126–131.)

# Finger Spelling Double L Words

**Getting Ready:** Teach students the finger spellings for the letters *e*, *i*, *u*, and *l*. (*Note:* The letter *a* is not used because the word family *-all* does not have a short vowel sound.)

e          i          u          l

**Directions:** Name a double *L* word. Refer to the list in the activity above. For example, say the word *bell* and then begin to spell the word by calling out the initial consonant (*b*). Have students make the finger spellings for the remaining letters in the word (*ell*). Repeat the activity with other words as time and interest allow.

# Roll and Rhyme Sort: "Tick-Tack-Tock" Game

**Getting Ready:** Print the words *tick*, *tack*, and *"tock"* on 5" x 8" (13 cm x 20 cm) index cards using a red marker. On each additional index card, print one of the following words with a black marker: *back, black\*, block\*, brick\*, chick\*, clock\*, crack, dock, flick, flock, frock, hock, jack\*, kick\*, lack, lick, lock\*, mock, pack\*, pick, quick\*, rock\*, sack, shack, shock, sick\*, slick, smack, smock, snack\*, sock, stick, tack, thick, track, and trick.* Copy the die pattern on page 143 onto colorful card stock and cut it out along the dashed lines. Fold the pattern along the solid lines to form a cube shape. Glue the tabs as indicated on the die.

**Directions:**

1. Show the cards to students and read the words out loud. Have students also take turns reading the words orally. Talk about the word families that are represented. Point out how the letter cluster *ck* stands for the /k/ sound.
2. Ask three students to hold up the large words printed in red (*tick*, *tack*, and *tock*) in front of the class. Choose a student to be the caller for the game. Have the remaining students form three teams. Give each team four cards from each word family for a total of 12 cards.
3. Direct each team to sort its cards and then stack the words faceup in three piles. For each round of play, one player on each team is designated as the "walker."

**How to Play:** The caller rolls the paper die and then reads the word aloud. Each team looks for one word that rhymes with the specified word and then sends that word card with its walker to the front of the class. The walker reads the team's word choice out loud and stands near the corresponding rhyming word written in red. If the word choice is correct, that team earns a point. The word card is discarded with the caller and the walker returns to the team. If the word choice is incorrect, the walker brings the word card back to the team. Continue playing until a team no longer has any cards for one of the word families.

**Culmination:** Select the words you would like to add to the "'Splish, Splash,' Word Fun" bulletin-board word wall and print them on small index cards that have been cut in half. Label the word families on the appropriate shapes and include them with the words. (*Note*: Words above marked with an asterisk are provided on pages 126–131.)

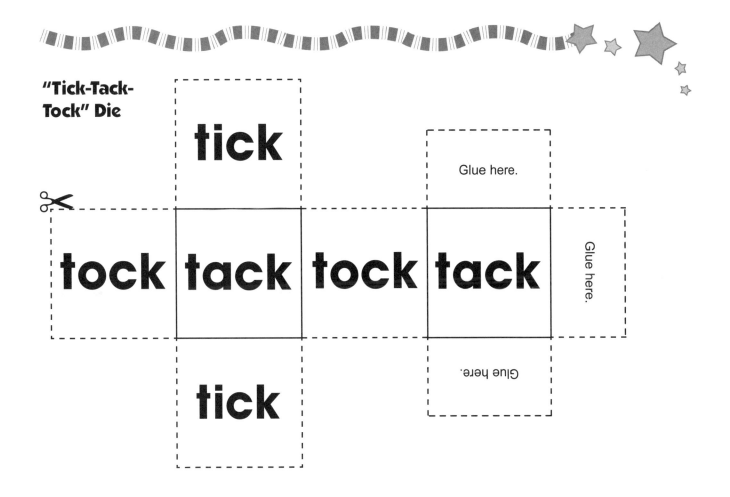

# More Word Turners

**Getting Ready:** Have students print the letters *b*, *c*, *d*, *f*, *p*, *s*, and *t* individually on index cards.

**Directions:** Write the word *and* on the board. Ask, "Which letter turns *and* into *band*?" Have students look at their letter cards and hold up the letter that best completes the word. Choose one student to come forward and print the letter *b* in front of the word *and*. Repeat the steps with the other questions.

Which letter turns *lack* into *black*?
Which letter turns *lend* into *blend*?
Which letter turns *ramp* into *cramp*?
Which letter turns *lash* into *clash*?
Which letter turns *well* into *dwell*?
Which letter turns *lash* into *slash*?
Which letter turns *rash* into *trash**?
Which letter turns *last* into *blast**?
Which letter turns *lick* into *flick*?
Which letter turns *ring** into *bring**?

Which letter turns *lamp** into *clamp*?
Which letter turns *rank* into *prank*?
Which letter turns *land* into *bland*?
Which letter turns *mash* into *smash**?
Which letter turns *less* into *bless*?
Which letter turns *end* into *send**?
Which letter turns *elf* into *self*?
Which letter turns *peck* into *speck*?
Which letter turns *rift* into *drift*?
Which letter turns *luck** into *cluck*?

**Culmination:** Select the words you would like to add to the "'Splish, Splash,' Word Fun" bulletin-board word wall and print them on small index cards that have been cut in half. Label the word families on the appropriate shapes and include them with the words. (*Note*: Words above marked with an asterisk are provided on pages 126–131.)

# Changing Words

**Directions:** Have students write the numbers 1–10 on their papers. One at a time, print a word (words listed below) on the board and then provide the directions for changing it into a new word. Have students record the new words on their papers. Choose a student to name each new word and list the correct answers on the board.

**Optional:** Direct students to listen for specific sounds instead of saying the names of the letters. For example, say the word *band*. Ask students to change the /b/ to /s/ to make the new word. (*sand*)

## Set A

1. *band\**—Change the letter *b* to *s*. What is the new word? (*sand\**)
2. *cash\**—Change the letter *c* to *d*. What is the new word? (*dash*)
3. *wing*—Change the letter *w* to *r*. What is the new word? (*ring\**)
4. *sank\**—Change the letter *s* to *b*. What is the new word? (*bank*)
5. *bill\**—Change the letter *b* to *f*. What is the new word? (*fill\**)
6. *best\**—Change the letter *b* to *r*. What is the new word? (*rest*)
7. *jack\**—Change the letter *j* to *t*. What is the new word? (*tack*)
8. *dock*—Change the letter *d* to *s*. What is the new word? (*sock*)
9. *sink\**—Change the letter *s* to *w*. What is the new word? (*wink*)
10. *buck\**—Change the letter *b* to *d*. What is the new word? (*duck\**)

## Set B

1. *vest\**—Change the letter *v* to *n*. What is the new word? (*nest*)
2. *rank*—Change the letter *r* to *y*. What is the new word? (*yank*)
3. *lick*—Change the letter *l* to *s*. What is the new word? (*sick\**)
4. *mend*—Change the letter *m* to *b*. What is the new word? (*bend\**)
5. *pill*—Change the letter *p* to *h*. What is the new word? (*hill\**)
6. *must\**—Change the letter *m* to *d*. What is the new word? (*dust\**)
7. *pink\**—Change the letter *p* to *r*. What is the new word? (*rink*)
8. *sack*—Change the letter *s* to *b*. What is the new word? (*back\**)
9. *rock\**—Change the letter *r* to *l*. What is the new word? (*lock\**)
10. *past\**—Change the letter *p* to *f*. What is the new word? (*fast\**)

## Set C

1. *pest*—Change the letter *p* to *z*. What is the new word? (*zest*)
2. *bump*—Change the letter *b* to *j*. What is the new word? (*jump\**)
3. *pick*—Change the letter *p* to *k*. What is the new word? (*kick\**)
4. *king\**—Change the letter *k* to *s*. What is the new word? (*sing\**)
5. *fell\**—Change the letter *f* to *t*. What is the new word? (*tell*)
6. *dish\**—Change the letter *d* to *f*. What is the new word? (*fish\**)
7. *puff*—Change the letter *p* to *h*. What is the new word? (*huff*)
8. *sunk*—Change the letter *s* to *b*. What is the new word? (*bunk\**)
9. *less*—Change the letter *l* to *m*. What is the new word? (*mess\**)
10. *bank*—Change the letter *b* to *t*. What is the new word? (*tank\**)

(*Note*: Words marked with an asterisk are provided on pages 126–131.)

# Rhyming Twins Word Hunt

**Getting Ready:** Make a copy of the Rhyming Twins Word Hunt lists on page 146 for each student.

**Directions:**

1. On the board, one word at a time, list the first word of each rhyming word pair. Select those words that are appropriate for your students. The answers for Word List B are shown in parentheses.

| | | |
|---|---|---|
| band, sand*, (hand*) | glass*, pass*, (class*) | elf, shelf, (self) |
| sting, fling, (ring*) | hint*, print*, (mint*) | stick, brick*, (quick*) |
| bath, path, (math) | neck*, check*, (speck) | smock, block*, (clock*) |
| stomp, chomp | chimp*, limp*, (blimp) | luck*, truck*, (duck*) |
| fast*, past*, (blast*) | loft, soft | blink*, drink*, (sink*) |
| bond, pond, (fond) | lend, mend, (bend*) | twist*, fist*, (list*) |
| less, mess*, (bless) | spell*, dwell, (swell) | wish*, dish*, (fish*) |
| gift*, lift*, (drift) | plump*, grump, (jump*) | sank*, blank*, (thank*) |
| rung*, stung*, (flung*) | brush*, crush*, (hush*) | damp, stamp*, (camp) |
| chest*, vest*, (best*) | junk*, skunk*, (shrunk) | crept*, kept*, (slept) |
| rash, cash*, (smash*) | sent, spent*, (rent*) | cuff*, stuff*, (muff) |
| pack*, snack*, (back*) | chill, still*, (hill*) | rang*, sang*, (bang*) |

2. Say the given word. Direct students to look on their sheets (List A) to find the rhyming word.
3. Have students take turns coming to the board to list the rhyming words. *Note*: The game may be played again at a different time by using List B words.

**Culmination:** Select the words you would like to add to the "'Splish, Splash,' Word Fun" bulletin-board word wall and print them on small index cards that have been cut in half. (*Note*: Words above marked with an asterisk are provided on **pages 126–131**.)

# Make-a-Rhyme Memory Match

**Getting Ready:** Copy page 147 for each pair of students. On the board, list the first word of each rhyming triplet below:

| | |
|---|---|
| list*, mist, twist* | camp, champ*, lamp* |
| fleck, deck*, neck* | sang*, clang, hang |
| tend, spend*, blend | mast, last, cast |
| stuff*, bluff*, gruff* | pump, dump*, slump* |
| kiss, hiss, miss | press, dress*, chess* |

**Directions:** Pair the students. Direct them to look at their word sheets and find two rhyming words for each word on the board. When everyone is finished, have students take turns naming the rhyming words. Print their answers on the board.

**How to Play:** Have students cut out the word cards along the dashed lines. Direct students to arrange their cards facedown in the center of the playing area and then take turns looking at two cards to find the matching pairs of words. If the chosen cards cannot be matched, the cards are returned facedown for the next player's turn. Continue in this manner until all cards have been matched.

**Culmination:** Follow the directions provided in the previous activity for the bulletin-board word wall.

Directions on page 145

# Word List A: Rhyming Twins Word Hunt

- ☐ blank
- ☐ block
- ☐ brick
- ☐ cash
- ☐ check
- ☐ chomp
- ☐ crush
- ☐ dish
- ☐ drink
- ☐ dwell
- ☐ fist
- ☐ fling
- ☐ grump
- ☐ kept
- ☐ lift
- ☐ limp
- ☐ mend
- ☐ mess
- ☐ pass
- ☐ past
- ☐ path
- ☐ pond
- ☐ print
- ☐ sand
- ☐ sang
- ☐ shelf
- ☐ skunk
- ☐ snack
- ☐ soft
- ☐ spent
- ☐ stamp
- ☐ still
- ☐ stuff
- ☐ stung
- ☐ truck
- ☐ vest

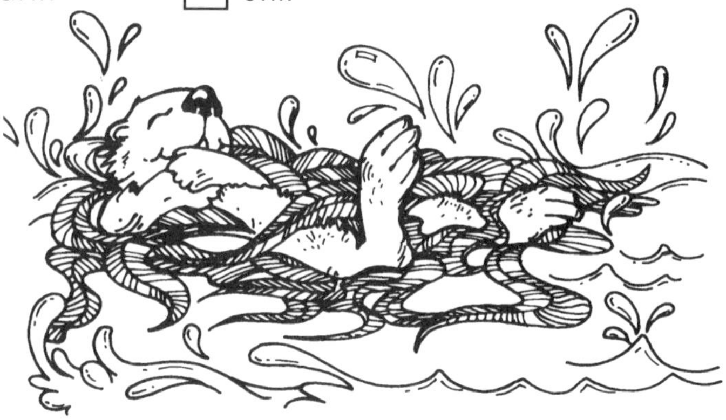

# Word List B: Rhyming Twins Word Hunt

- ☐ back
- ☐ bang
- ☐ bend
- ☐ best
- ☐ blast
- ☐ bless
- ☐ blimp
- ☐ camp
- ☐ class
- ☐ clock
- ☐ drift
- ☐ duck
- ☐ fish
- ☐ flung
- ☐ fond
- ☐ hand
- ☐ hill
- ☐ hush
- ☐ jump
- ☐ list
- ☐ math
- ☐ mint
- ☐ muff
- ☐ quick
- ☐ rent
- ☐ ring
- ☐ self
- ☐ shrunk
- ☐ sink
- ☐ slept
- ☐ smash
- ☐ speck
- ☐ swell
- ☐ thank

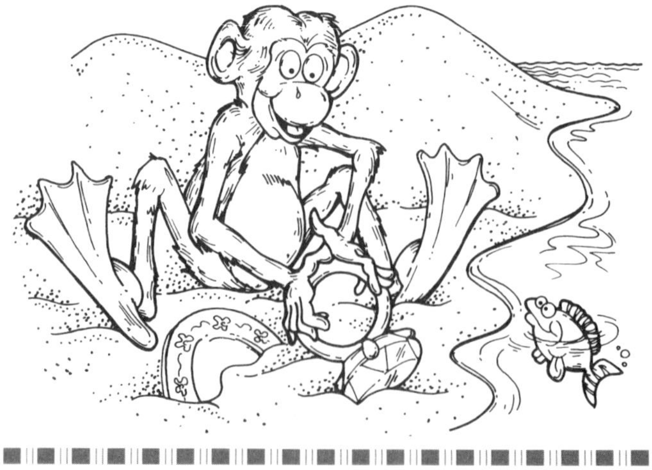

| | | | |
|---|---|---|---|
| chess | miss | neck | hiss |
| champ | fast | mist | twist |
| bluff | dump | last | spend |
| blend | dress | lamp | slump |
| hang | deck | gruff | clang |

# Making Little Words

**Getting Ready:** For each group of two or three players, you will need the four dice on pages 149 and 151, scissors, and glue. Copy the dice patterns onto colorful card stock and cut them out along the dashed lines. Fold each pattern along the solid lines to form a cube shape. Glue the tabs as indicated on the dice. Make a copy of the recording sheet on page 152 for each player.

**How to Play:** In each group, players take turns rolling the dice (Dice A, B, E, and F) and then writing the indicated letters (consonants and consonant clusters) in separate boxes on their recording sheets. Continue in this manner until each player has filled in all boxes on his sheet. How many words can students spell? The players can only combine the letters in a column with that column's vowel heading to spell a CVC or CVCC word. Letters can be used more than one time. For example, if a player has written the letters *t*, *ll*, and *w* in the *e* column, then the words *tell* and *well* can be spelled. Have the players record their words on the lines. If more space is needed, the words can also be written on the backs of the sheets. You may wish to encourage students to use the bulletin-board word wall as a resource when generating words. (Remind children that those words that are considered to be "bad" should not be used.) At the end of a predetermined time, have the players check their lists to find out who generated the most words. Alternatively, two points could be awarded for each word that only appears on one player's list.

**Optional Play:** For struggling readers, it may be appropriate for them to spell CVC words by generating letter choices with Dice A and B only. If your students need to be challenged, you may consider providing them with all six dice (see pages 149–151) so that they may spell CCVC and CCVCC words, too.

# Word Maker

**Getting Ready:** For each group of two to four players, you will need the four dice on pages 149 and 150, scissors, and glue. Copy the dice patterns onto colorful card stock and cut them out along the dashed lines. Fold each pattern along the solid lines to form a cube shape. Glue the tabs as indicated on the dice. Make a copy of the game boards on pages 153–156 for each group.

**How to Play:** Have each player select a game board. In each group, players take turns rolling the dice (Dice A and B) and then writing the indicated letters in separate boxes on their boards. Continue in this manner until each player has filled in all boxes on her board. Now, challenge the players to generate words with the letters. How many words can they spell? The players can only combine the letters in a column with that column's word-family heading to spell the words. Letters can be used more than one time. For example, if the player using Board #1 has written the letters *t*, *c*, and *r* under the *-ack* column, then the words *tack*, *track*, and *crack* can all be spelled. Have the players record their words on the lines. If more space is needed, the words can also be written on the backs of the game boards. Make your students aware of more words than they can quickly recall by having them use the bulletin-board word wall as a reference tool. (Remind children that those words that are considered to be "bad" should not be used.) At the end of a predetermined time, have the players check their lists to find out who generated the most words. Alternatively, two points could be awarded for each word that only appears on one player's list.

**Optional Play:** Have students generate words by using Dice A, B, C, and D. Then, they can spell words with initial consonant clusters, too.

# Die A

# Die B

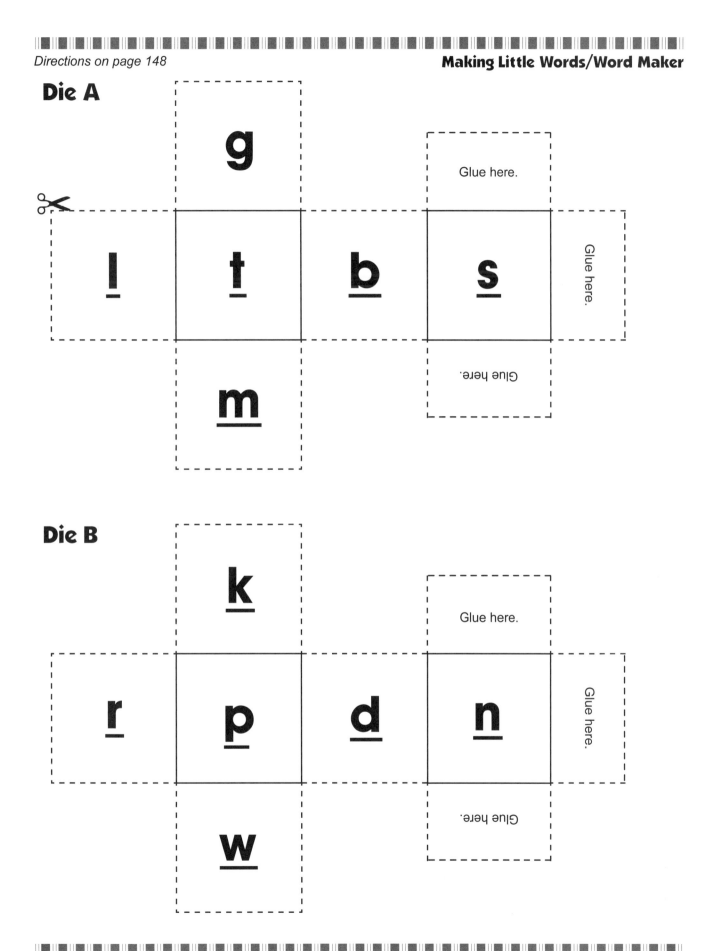

**Die C**
**Beginning**
**Consonant**
**Clusters**

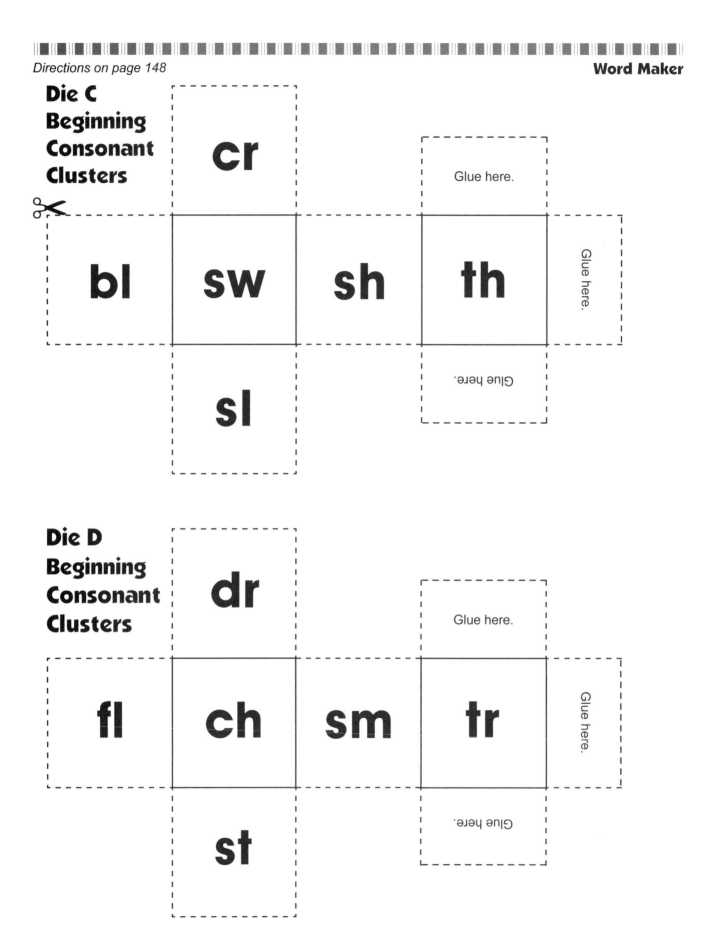

cr

Glue here.

Glue here.

bl sw sh th

Glue here.

sl

**Die D**
**Beginning**
**Consonant**
**Clusters**

dr

Glue here.

Glue here.

fl ch sm tr

Glue here.

st

**Die E
Final
Consonant
Clusters**

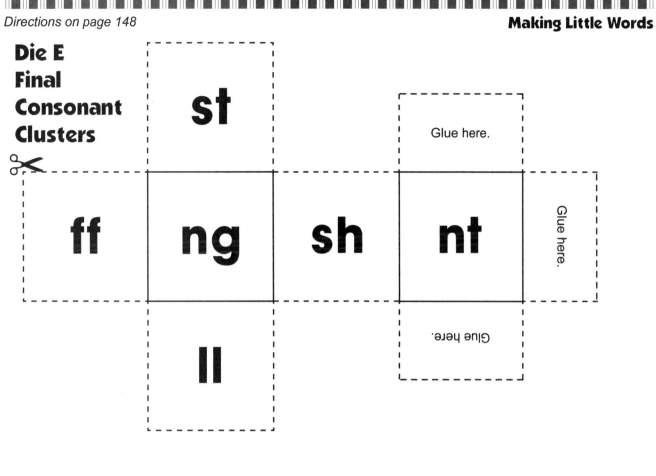

st

ff  ng  sh  nt

Glue here.

Glue here.

Glue here.

ll

**Die F
Final
Consonant
Clusters**

mp

nd  ck  ft  nk

Glue here.

Glue here.

Glue here.

st

# Making Little Words

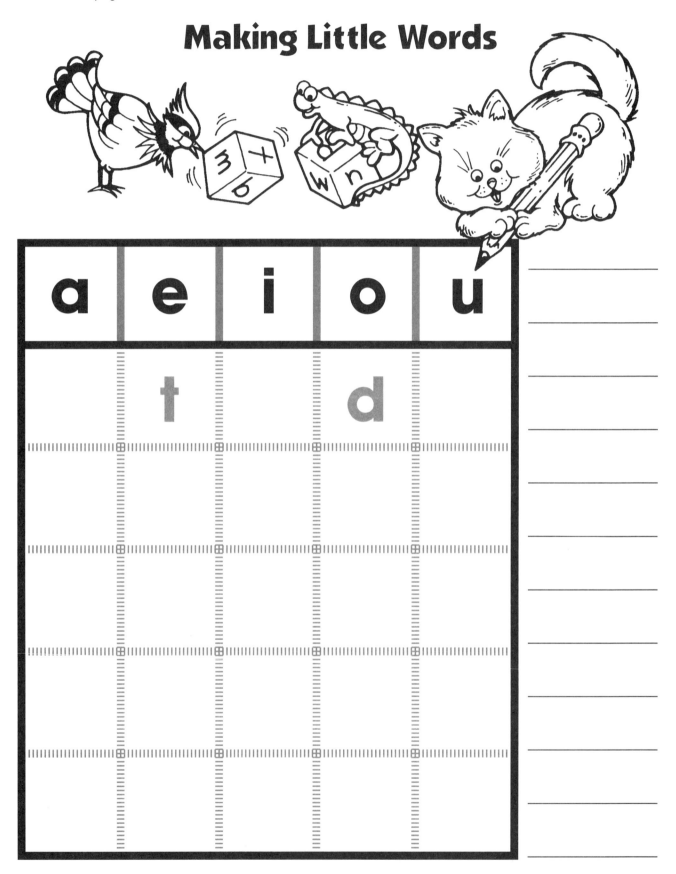

| a | e | i | o | u |
|---|---|---|---|---|
|   | t |   | d |   |

# Word Maker

### Board #1

| _ack | _ell | _ing | _ink | _ust |
|------|------|------|------|------|
|      |      |      |      |      |
|      |      |      |      |      |
|      |      |      |      |      |
|      |      |      |      |      |

# Word Maker

### Board #2

| _ank | _ess | _est | _ick | _ump |
|------|------|------|------|------|

*Directions on page 148*

# Word Maker

### Board #3

| _ash | _end | _ock | _ull | _unk |
|------|------|------|------|------|
|      |      |      |      |      |

# Word Maker

## Board #4

| _and | _ent | _ill | _uck | _uff |
|------|------|------|------|------|

# Roll and Read Words

**Getting Ready:** For each group of two to four players, you will need five dice, scissors, and glue. Copy the dice patterns on pages 59 and 149 onto white card stock and page 151 onto blue or red card stock to make the final consonant clusters easy to identify. Cut out the dice patterns along the dashed lines. Fold each pattern along the solid lines to form a cube shape. Glue the tabs as indicated on the die. Also, copy the word list below for the players.

**How to Play:** In each group, players take turns rolling all five of the dice. The player attempts to spell a word(s) with the vowel, initial consonants, and consonant clusters indicated and then writes the words on a sheet of paper. Example: *b, w, e, ll, nd—bell, well, bend.* The asterisk on the vowel die can be any vowel the student wishes to name. Students may also refer to the word list below when trying to build words. At the end of the predetermined time or a specified number of rounds, the player with the most words is declared the winner.

 - - - - - - - - - - - - - - - - - - - - - - - - - - - - - - - - - - - - - - - - - - - -

## Roll and Read Words

**Examples include the following words:**

| | |
|---|---|
| **-ack:** back, lack, pack, rack, sack, tack | **-imp:** limp |
| **-amp:** damp, lamp | **-ing:** ding, king, ping, ring, sing, wing |
| **-and:** band, land, sand | |
| **-ang:** bang, pang, rang, sang | **-ink:** link, mink, pink, rink, sink, wink |
| **-ank:** bank, rank, sank, tank | **-int:** lint, mint, tint |
| **-ash:** dash, gash, mash, rash, sash | **-ish:** dish, wish |
| **-ast:** last, mast, past | **-ist:** list, mist |
| **-eck:** deck, neck, peck | **-ock:** dock, lock, mock, rock, sock |
| **-ell:** bell, dell, sell, tell, well | **-oft:** loft, soft |
| **-end:** bend, lend, mend, send, tend | **-ond:** bond, pond |
| **-ent:** bent, dent, lent, rent, sent, tent, went | **-uck:** buck, duck, luck, puck, tuck |
| | **-uff:** muff, puff |
| **-est:** best, nest, pest, rest, test, west | **-ump:** bump, dump, lump, pump |
| | **-ung:** lung, rung, sung |
| **-ick:** kick, lick, pick, sick, tick, wick | **-unk:** bunk, sunk |
| **-ift:** gift, lift, rift, sift | **-ush:** gush, lush, mush, rush |
| **-ill:** bill, dill, gill, mill, pill, sill, will | **-ust:** dust, gust, must |

# Long-Vowel Phonograms
## (CVVC, CVCe, CVCC, CCVV & CCVCC Words)
*Note*: Due to differences in dialects, certain word families may not have long-vowel sounds when spoken in your area.

## Long "a" Families

| -ace | -ail | -ain | -ake | -ame | -ane | -ate |
|------|------|------|------|------|------|------|
| face* | fail | brain* | bake* | blame* | cane* | date* |
| lace | jail | chain | brake | came | crane | gate* |
| pace | mail* | drain | cake* | fame | lane* | hate |
| place* | nail | main | lake | flame | mane | late |
| race* | pail | pain* | make | frame | plane* | plate |
| space | sail | rain* | rake | game* | | skate* |
| trace | snail* | | shake* | lame | | state |
| | tail* | **-ait** | snake | name* | **-ape** | |
| **-age** | trail | bait* | stake | same | ape* | **-ave** |
| age | | trait | take | | cape | cave |
| cage* | | wait* | wake* | | grape* | gave* |
| page* | | | | | shape | save* |
| wage | | | | | tape* | shave |
| stage* | | | | | | wave* |

## Long "e" Families

| -each | -eak | -eam | -eap | -eed | -eel | -eep |
|-------|------|------|------|------|------|------|
| beach* | beak* | beam* | cheap* | bleed | eel* | deep* |
| each | creak | cream | heap* | feed* | feel* | keep* |
| peach* | leak* | dream* | leap* | need* | heel* | peep |
| reach | sneak | seam | | seed* | peel | sheep* |
| teach* | speak* | steam | **-eat** | speed | steel | sleep |
| | weak | team* | beat* | weed | | steep |
| **-ead** | | | cheat | | **-een** | sweep |
| bead* | **-eal** | **-ean** | heat* | **-eek** | green* | weep |
| lead* | deal* | bean* | meat | cheek* | keen | |
| read* | meal | clean* | neat | peek* | queen* | **-eet** |
| | real* | dean | seat | seek | seen* | beet |
| **-eaf** | seal* | mean* | treat* | sleek | | feet* |
| leaf | steal | | | week* | | meet* |
| | zeal | *The word is already printed on a card. (See pages 165–173.)* | | | | greet* |

# Long "i" Families

| -ice | -ife | -ile | -ind | -ipe | -ire | -ise | -ive |
|------|------|------|------|------|------|------|------|
| dice | life | mile* | blind | gripe | fire* | rise | chive |
| lice | wife | pile* | find* | pipe* | hire* | wise | dive* |
| mice* |  | smile* | grind | ripe* | tire* |  | drive* |
| nice | **-igh** | tile | kind* | swipe* | wire | **-ite** | five |
| price* | high |  | mind* | wipe |  | bite* | hive* |
| rice* | sigh | **-ime** |  |  |  | kite* | jive |
| slice |  | chime* | **-ine** |  |  | mite | live |
|  | **-ike** | crime | dine* |  |  | quite* |  |
| **-ide** | bike* | dime* | fine |  |  | site |  |
| hide* | hike* | grime | line |  |  |  |  |
| ride* | like* | lime | mine |  |  |  |  |
| side | pike | slime | nine |  |  |  |  |
| slide |  | time* | pine* |  |  |  |  |
| tide |  |  | shine* |  |  |  |  |
| wide* |  |  | spine |  |  |  |  |

# Long "o" Families

| -oad | -oat | -oke | -ole | -ope |
|------|------|------|------|------|
| load* | boat* | broke* | hole* | cope* |
| road* | coat* | choke | mole* | hope* |
| toad* | float | joke* | pole | rope* |
|  | goat* | smoke* | stole* | slope |
| **-oak** | oat | spoke |  |  |
| croak |  | woke | **-ome** | **-ose** |
| oak* | **-ode** |  | dome* | chose |
| soak* | code* | **-old** | home* | close |
|  | mode | bold* |  | hose* |
| **-oal** | rode* | cold* | **-one** | nose* |
| coal* |  | fold | bone* | rose* |
| foal |  | gold* | cone* | those |
| goal* |  | hold | phone* |  |
|  |  | sold | stone* | **-ost** |
|  |  | told | zone | most |
|  |  |  |  | post |

# Long "u" Families

| -ube | -ule |
|------|------|
| cube* | mule* |
| tube* | rule* |
|  |  |
| **-ude** | **-une** |
| dude* | June* |
| rude* | prune* |
|  | tune* |
| **-ue** |  |
| blue* | **-use** |
| clue* | fuse* |
| due* | use* |
| glue* |  |
| true* | **-ute** |
|  | cute* |
|  | flute* |
|  | mute |

*The word is already printed on a card. (See pages 165–173.)*

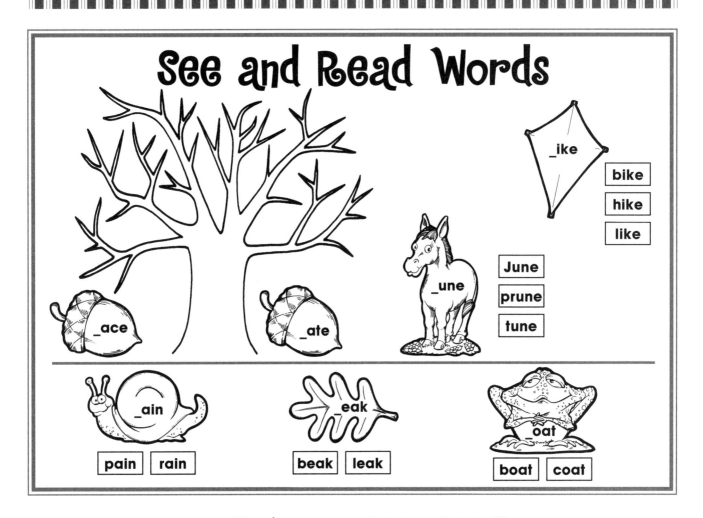

## Bulletin-Board Word Wall

**Getting Ready:** You will need sky-blue butcher paper, brown poster paint and a paintbrush, colorful card stock, markers, scissors, stapler, and patterns on pages 161–173.

**Directions:**
1. Begin by covering the bulletin board with paper. Arrange the paper so that the top of this display can be reached by standing children if you would like them to point to words.
2. Copy the title and decorative art on page 161 onto card stock. You may prefer to enlarge the art before making the reproductions. (Copy the title at 175% to make the lowercase letters about 3 in. [8 cm] in height.) Color the art as desired with markers and then cut out the individual pieces along the dashed lines. Staple the title in the center of the top of the board and other pieces where desired.
3. Draw and paint the shape of a large oak tree on the bulletin board.
4. Select the phonograms you will introduce and then make as many copies of the patterns on pages 162–164 on card stock as needed for displaying the word families. (You may wish to look at a photograph of a mule to see how to color it.) Also, copy the word cards on pages 165–173 onto card stock and cut them out.
5. Place all materials on a table by the board and then add the pieces to the display as new words are introduced during classroom activities.

**Read and see**

**See**

**and**

**Read**

**Words**

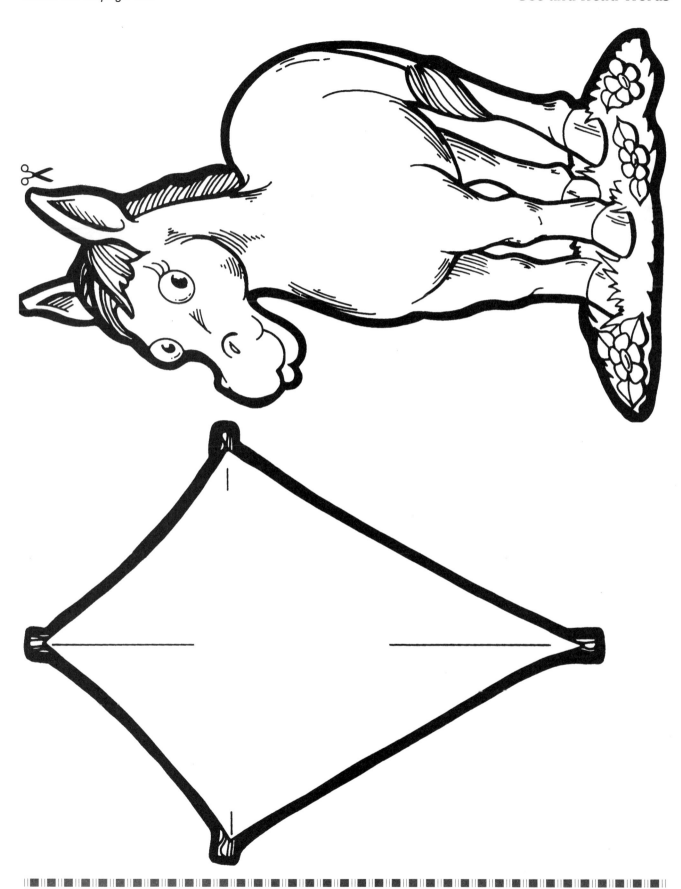

| face | place | race |
| cage | page | stage |
| mail | snail | tail |
| brain | pain | rain |
| bait | wait | bake |
| cake | shake | wake |

**165**

✂

| blame | game | name |
|-------|------|------|
| cane | lane | plane |
| ape | grape | tape |
| date | gate | skate |
| gave | save | wave |
| beach | peach | teach |

| bead | lead | read |
| --- | --- | --- |
| beak | leak | speak |
| deal | seal | real |
| beam | dream | team |
| bean | clean | mean |
| cheap | heap | leap |

| | | |
|---|---|---|
| **beat** | **heat** | **treat** |
| **feed** | **need** | **seed** |
| **cheek** | **peek** | **week** |
| **eel** | **feel** | **heel** |
| **green** | **queen** | **seen** |
| **deep** | **keep** | **sheep** |

| | | |
|---|---|---|
| **feet** | **meet** | **greet** |
| **mice** | **price** | **rice** |
| **hide** | **ride** | **wide** |
| **bike** | **hike** | **like** |
| **mile** | **pile** | **smile** |
| **chime** | **dime** | **time** |

| find | kind | mind |
| --- | --- | --- |
| dine | pine | shine |
| pipe | ripe | swipe |
| fire | hire | tire |
| bite | kite | quite |
| dive | drive | hive |

| load | road | toad |
|------|------|------|
| oak | soak | coal |
| goal | boat | coat |
| goat | code | rode |
| broke | joke | smoke |
| bold | cold | gold |

**171**

| hole | mole | stole |
|------|------|-------|
| dome | home | stone |
| bone | cone | phone |
| cope | hope | rope |
| hose | nose | rose |
| cube | tube | dude |

| rude | blue | clue |
| --- | --- | --- |
| due | glue | true |
| mule | rule | June |
| prune | tune | fuse |
| use | cute | flute |

# Changing Words

**Directions:** One at a time, say a word (words listed below) and then provide the directions for changing it into a new word. Ask students to tell you the new words.

**Optional:** Have students write the numbers 1–10 on their papers. One at a time, print a word (words listed below) on the board and then provide the directions for changing it into a new word by naming the letters. For example, read aloud the word *lace*. Ask students to change the *l* to *r* to make the new word (*race*). Have students record the new words on their papers. Choose a student to name each new word and list the correct answers on the board.

## Set A

1. *lace*—Change the sound /l/ to /r/. What is the new word? (*race**)
2. *cake**—Change the sound /k/ to /sh/. What is the new word? (*shake**)
3. *shape*—Change the sound /sh/ to /t/. What is the new word? (*tape**)
4. *need**—Change the sound /n/ to /f/. What is the new word? (*feed**)
5. *beet*—Change the sound /b/ to /m/. What is the new word? (*meet**)
6. *peek**—Change the sound /p/ to /ch/. What is the new word? (*cheek**)
7. *fine*—Change the sound /f/ to /l/. What is the new word? (*line*)
8. *live*—Change the sound /l/ to /j/. What is the new word? (*jive*)
9. *tide*—Change the sound /t/ to /s/. What is the new word? (*side*)
10. *sold*—Change the sound /s/ to /h/. What is the new word? (*hold*)

## Set B

1. *tune**—Change the sound /t/ to /j/. What is the new word? (*June**)
2. *tone*—Change the sound /t/ to /z/. What is the new word? (*zone*)
3. *dean*—Change the sound /d/ to /b/. What is the new word? (*bean**)
4. *bead**—Change the sound /b/ to /r/. What is the new word? (*read**)
5. *joke**—Change the sound /j/ to /w/. What is the new word? (*woke*)
6. *home**—Change the sound /h/ to /d/. What is the new word? (*dome**)
7. *leap**—Change the sound /l/ to /ch/. What is the new word? (*cheap**)
8. *came*—Change the sound /k/ to /f/. What is the new word? (*fame*)
9. *fake*—Change the sound /f/ to /l/. What is the new word? (*lake*)
10. *cute**—Change the sound /k/ to /m/. What is the new word? (*mute*)

## Set C

1. *meal*—Change the sound /m/ to /d/. What is the new word? (*deal**)
2. *neat*—Change the sound /n/ to /h/. What is the new word? (*heat**)
3. *rain**—Change the sound /r/ to /ch/. What is the new word? (*chain*)
4. *tail**—Change the sound /t/ to /p/. What is the new word? (*pail*)
5. *cave*—Change the sound /k/ to /g/. What is the new word? (*gave**)
6. *team**—Change the sound /t/ to /b/. What is the new word? (*beam**)
7. *fire**—Change the sound /f/ to /w/. What is the new word? (*wire*)
8. *bite**—Change the sound /b/ to /k/. What is the new word? (*kite**)
9. *coal**—Change the sound /k/ to /g/. What is the new word? (*goal**)
10. *bike**—Change the sound /b/ to /h/. What is the new word? (*hike**)

(*Note*: Words marked with an asterisk are provided on pages 165–173.)

# The Long Vowel Song

**Directions:** Teach students "The Long Vowel Song," sung to the tune of "The Wheels on the Bus Go 'Round and 'Round." *Note*: "The Short Vowel Song" is provided on page 132.

> Long **a** in a word goes /ā/ - /ā/ - /ā/, (Sing long a sound as in ape.)
> /ā/ - /ā/ - /ā/,
> /ā/ - /ā/ - /ā/.
> Long **a** in a word goes /ā/ - /ā/ - /ā/
> In all long **a** words!

Repeat the song with a verse for each long vowel sound.

# Loud A–Silent E or I

**Getting Ready:** On the board, print two sets of words: (List A) *bake\*, cage\*, cake\*, came, cane\*, cave, date\*, fake, game\*, gate\*, gave\*, lake, make, mane, name\*, rake, save\*, skate\*, take, tape\*, wake\*,* and *wave\*;* and (List B) *brain\*, mail\*, pail, pain\*, rain\*, sail,* and *tail.*

**Directions:**
1. Begin by explaining that often when a four-letter word has the vowel *e* at the end, the *e* is silent and the other vowel is long. Say the words and have students listen for the vowel sounds.
2. Complete a spelling action activity. As you point to words, have students spell them like this: speak the first letter, say the long *a* sound loudly, speak the sound for the third letter, and put index finger to pursed lips to indicate no sound for the letter *E*.
3. Repeat the actions for the *AI* words. Have children speak the sounds for the first and last letters, say the long *a* sound loudly, and indicate silence for the letter *I*.

**Culmination:** Select the words you would like to add to the "See and Read Words" bulletin-board word wall and print them on small index cards that have been cut in half. Label the word families on the appropriate shapes and include them with the words. (*Note*: Words above marked with an asterisk are on pages 165–173.)

# Egads! EEK!

**Getting Ready:** Print the letters *d, f, g, j, k, l, m, n, p, r, s, t,* and *w* individually on index cards. Depending upon the number of students in your class, make enough additional cards labeled with the double *e* so everyone will have a letter card. On the board, list these words: *deed, deep\*, feed\*, feel\*, feet\*, green\*, greet\*, keep\*, meet\*, need\*, peep, seed\*, seek, seen\*, sleep, speed, steep, weed, week\*,* and *weep.*

**Directions:** Select a word randomly from the list. One at a time, a student comes forward to spell the selected word. Ask, "Who do you need to help you spell [name of word]? Have the student name two or three other children who come forward. Arrange the students in order to spell the word. Invite the class to say the word. Repeat the steps for each word.

**Culmination:** Follow the directions in the previous activity for the bulletin-board word wall.

# Teamwork

**Getting Ready:** For each pair of students, you will need 10 small index cards. On the board, list the following long vowel words: *beak\**, *beam\**, *bean\**, *beat\**, *dean*, *lead\**, *leaf*, *leak\**, *meal*, *mean\**, *meat*, *neat*, *read\**, *real\**, *seal\**, *seam*, *seat*, *steal*, and *team\**. In addition, draw the picture code shown below on the board for students to see.

ea = (picture)    b = (picture)    d = (picture)    f = (picture)    l = (picture)

m = (picture)    n = (picture)    r = (picture)    s = (picture)    t = (picture)    k = (picture)

**Directions:** Pair the students and give each team 10 index cards. Students are to write one of the listed words in code by drawing pictures on the front of each card and then print the actual word on the back. Have students exchange their cards with another team and solve the codes.

**Culmination:** Select the words you would like to add to the "See and Read Words" bulletin-board word wall and print them on small index cards that have been cut in half. Label the word families on the appropriate shapes and include them with the words. (*Note*: Words above marked with an asterisk are provided on pages 165–173.)

# Which Sound: Long *i* or Long *o*?

**Getting Ready:** On the board, list the following long vowel words—*bike\**, *bite\**, *bone\**, *cold\**, *cone\**, *dime\**, *fine*, *goat\**, *hide\**, *high*, *hold*, *home\**, *hose\**, *joke\**, *lice*, *life*, *like\**, *lime*, *live*, *mile\**, *mind\**, *most*, *pine\**, *pipe\**, *poke*, *post*, *ride\**, *ripe\**, *rise*, *rope\**, *rose\**, *tile*, and *tone*.

**Directions:** One at a time, say the words in random order. Students indicate the vowel sound by pointing their index fingers for the long *i* sound and using index fingers and thumbs to make circles for the long *o* sound. Choose a student to find the word on the list.

**Culmination:** Follow the directions in the previous activity for the bulletin-board word wall.

# Missing Vowels

**Getting Ready:** On the board, list the following words with a vowel (underlined) missing: *k*i*nd\**, *t*u*ne\**, *b*oa*t\**, *c*oa*t\**, *J*u*ne*, *m*o*ld*, *s*o*ld*, *t*o*ld*, *b*o*ld\**, *t*u*be\**, *w*i*se*, *r*i*ce\**, *tr*u*e\**, and *f*o*ld*. For example, write *k__nd* for the word *kind*.

**Directions:** One at a time, say the words in order. Have students take turns naming the missing vowel and coming to the board to write the letter in the blank.

**Culmination:** Follow the directions in the first activity above for the bulletin-board word wall.

# What Do You Hear?

**Getting Ready:** For each group of five students, prepare five small index cards by writing one of the vowels (*a*, *e*, *i*, *o*, and *u*) on each card. On the board, select 15–20 of the following words: *blue\*, broke\*, cape, choke, clue,\* crane, code\*, cope\*, croak, cube\*, dive\*, face\*, file, find\*, five, float, flute\*, grape\*, hole\*, June\*, lane\*, load\*, mice\*, mine, mole\*, nice, nine, nose\*, page\*, pile\*, place\*, plane\*, pole, race\*, rode\*, rule\*, slide, smile\*, soak\*, stole\*, stone\*, swipe\*, tide, time\*, tire\*, toad\*, use\*, wide\*, wife*, and *wipe*. You may be interested in repeating this activity with the words that have not been used.

**Directions:** Give each student a vowel card. In random order, say the words one at a time. For each word, ask, "What vowel do you hear?" Students with the appropriate vowel cards hold them up. Ask, "Is there another vowel in the word?" Students with this vowel hold their cards up. Ask, "Is the second vowel long, short, or silent?" Repeat with another word.

**Culmination:** Select the words you would like to add to the "See and Read" bulletin-board word wall and print them on small index cards that have been cut in half. Label the word families on the appropriate shapes and include them with the words. (*Note*: Words above marked with an asterisk are provided on pages 165–173.)

# Unscramble Relay

**Directions:** Review the fact that many four-letter words with two vowels have a silent *e*. Give examples such as *bike*, *bone*, and *five*.

**How to Play:**
1. Divide the class into two or three teams.
2. On the board, one at a time, write a scrambled word from the word list below.

**Scrambled Words:**

| | | |
|---|---|---|
| mide (*dime\**) | veac (*cave*) | piwe (*wipe*) |
| vdei (*dive\**) | deam (*made*) | emit (*time\**) |
| edaf (*fade*) | dihe (*hide\**) | lcei (*lice*) |
| kile (*like\**) | meoh (*home\**) | ealk (*lake*) |
| ibet (*bite\**) | seoh (*hose\**) | ciem (*mice\**) |
| oenb (*bone\**) | noec (*cone\**) | paet (*tape\**) |
| kare (*rake*) | poeh (*hope\**) | prie (*ripe\**) |
| nife (*fine*) | tdae (*date\**) | lope (*pole*) |
| iefv (*five*) | ughe (*huge*) | ones (*nose\**) |
| aegc (*cage\**) | oser (*rose\**) | emas (*same*) |

3. One member from each team will race to the board and try to unscramble the word. The first team to unscramble each word earns a point. Keep score on the board. The team with the highest score is declared the winner.

**Bonus:** Challenge students to make two different words from these letter combinations.

| eamt (*team, meat*) | ilfe (*file, life*) | liem (*mile, lime*) | eont (*note, tone*) |

**Culmination:** Follow the directions in the previous activity for the bulletin-board word wall.

# Change the Vowel

**Directions:** One at a time, print a long vowel word (words listed below) on the board and then provide the directions for changing it into a new word. Have students write the new word on their papers.

1. *bake*\*—Change the long vowel to spell *bike*\*.
2. *race*\*—Change the long vowel to spell *rice*\*.
3. *rise*—Change the long vowel to spell *rose*\*.
4. *tone*—Change the long vowel to spell *tune*\*.
5. *like*\*—Change the long vowel to spell *lake*.
6. *cane*\*—Change the long vowel to spell *cone*\*.
7. *pope*—Change the long vowel to spell *pipe*\*.
8. *mane*—Change the long vowel to spell *mine*.
9. *ripe*\*—Change the long vowel to spell *rope*\*.
10. *lane*\*—Change the long vowel to spell *line*.

**Culmination:** Select the words you would like to add to the "See and Read" bulletin-board word wall and print them on small index cards that have been cut in half. Label the word families on the appropriate shapes and include them with the words. (*Note*: Words above marked with an asterisk are provided on pages 165–173.)

# Try These Word Turners

**Getting Ready:** Print the letters *b*, *d*, *f*, *g*, *h*, *k*, *l*, *m*, *n*, *p*, *r*, *s*, *t*, and *w* individually on index cards. Prepare enough cards so that each student has a letter.

**Directions:** Write *see* on the board. Ask, "What letter turns *see* into *seed*?" The student holding the letter *d* should come forward and place the card after the word *see*. Choose a student to read the new word. Repeat the steps with other questions listed below:

Which letter turns *see* into *seek*?
Which letter turns *ate* into *rate*?
Which letter turns *oat* into *boat*\*?
Which letter turns *see* into *seen*\*?
Which letter turns *fee* into *feed*\*?
Which letter turns *fee* into *feel*\*?
Which letter turns *wee* into *weed*?
Which letter turns *ice* into *nice*?
Which letter turns *ate* into *date*\*?
Which letter turns *age* into *page*\*?
Which letter turns *eat* into *seat*?
Which letter turns *old* into *gold*\*?
Which letter turns *old* into *bold*\*?
Which letter turns *ail* into *sail*?
Which letter turns *old* into *hold*?
Which letter turns *ate* into *late*?

Which letter turns *ate* into *gate*\*?
Which letter turns *eat* into *beat*\*?
Which letter turns *see* into *seen*\*?
Which letter turns *ail* into *mail*\*?
Which letter turns *old* into *told*?
Which letter turns *fee* into *feet*\*?
Which letter turns *wee* into *weep*?
Which letter turns *ice* into *mice*\*?
Which letter turns *ice* into *rice*\*?
Which letter turns *eel* into *heel*\*?
Which letter turns *eat* into *meat*?
Which letter turns *eel* into *peel*?
Which letter turns *old* into *fold*?
Which letter turns *age* into *wage*?
Which letter turns *wee* into *week*?
Which letter turns *see* into *seed*\*?

**Culmination:** Follow the directions in the previous activity for the bulletin-board word wall.

# More Word Turners

**Getting Ready:** Have students print the letters *b, c, d, f, g, p, s,* and *t* individually on index cards.

**Directions:** Write the word *age* on the board. Ask, "Which letter turns *age* into *cage*?" Each student holds up the letter card that best completes the word. Choose one student to come forward and print the letter *c* in front of the word *age*. Repeat the steps with other questions listed below.

Which letter turns *nail* into *snail*\*?
Which letter turns *ape\** into *cape*?
Which letter turns *oat* into *goat*\*?
Which letter turns *lane\** into *plane\**?
Which letter turns *lame* into *blame\**?
Which letter turns *pace* into *space*?
Which letter turns *each* into *beach\**?
Which letter turns *poke* into *spoke*?
Which letter turns *weep* into *sweep*?

Which letter turns *lame* into *flame*?
Which letter turns *each* into *peach\**?
Which letter turns *late* into *plate*?
Which letter turns *take* into *stake*?
Which letter turns *ripe\** into *gripe*?
Which letter turns *eel\** into *feel\**?
Which letter turns *ice* into *dice*?
Which letter turns *each* into *teach\**?
Which letter turns *ape\** into *tape\**?

**Culmination:** Select the words you would like to add to the "See and Read Words" bulletin-board word wall and print them on small index cards that have been cut in half. Label the word families on the appropriate shapes and include them with the words. (*Note*: Words above marked with an asterisk are provided on pages 165–173.)

# I See a Word

**Getting Ready:** If the words featured below are not already displayed on the "See and Read Words" bulletin-board word wall, print them on small index cards that have been cut in half and place them in the appropriate locations.

**Directions:** Meet at the bulletin-board word wall to play a guessing game. Give clues to a mystery word. Students may either spell the answers or point to the words on the board.

**Examples:**
1. I see a word. It begins with the sound /r/ and rhymes with *toad*. (*road*)
2. I see a word. It begins with the sound /k/ and rhymes with *sleep*. (*keep*)
3. I see a word that rhymes with *weed*. It begins with the sound /s/. (*seed*)
4. I see two words that rhyme with *dime*. (*lime, time, etc.*)
5. I see a number word that rhymes with *live*. (*five*)
6. I see the name of a vegetable that begins with the sound /b/. (*bean*)
7. I see the name of a container that could be used for carrying water. (*pail*)
8. I see a word that rhyme with *mail* and begins with the sound /s/. (*sail*)
9. I see a word that rhymes with *greet* and begins with the sound /f/. (*feet*)
10. I see four words that rhyme with *side*. (*hide, ride, tide, wide, etc.*)

# Vowel Team Word Wheel

**Getting Ready:** For each student, copy the word wheels on pages 181 and 182 onto colorful card stock. In addition, each student will need a small paper plate, glue, scissors, and a brad.

**Directions:** Have students make their own wheels.
1.  Cut out the wheels and glue the largest wheel onto the center of a small paper plate.
2.  Stack the medium-sized wheel and then smallest one on the paper plate. Fasten the three wheels together in the center with a brad in such a way that the wheels turn.

**How to Play:** One at a time, read the words below in random order. Have students line up the letters to spell each word and then show the results. Check off each word as it is spelled.

**Culmination:** Select the words you would like to add to the "See and Read Words" bulletin-board word wall and print them on small index cards that have been cut in half. Label the word families on the appropriate shapes and include them with the words. (*Note*: Words below marked with an asterisk are provided on pages 165–173.)

✂ - - - - - - - - - - - - - - - - - - - - - - - - - - - - - - - - - -

# Word List for Word Wheel

| | | | | |
|---|---|---|---|---|
| ☐ beach* | ☐ feed* | ☐ leap* | ☐ peek* | ☐ seem |
| ☐ bead* | ☐ feel* | ☐ load* | ☐ peel | ☐ seen* |
| ☐ beak* | ☐ feet* | ☐ mail* | ☐ rain* | ☐ soak* |
| ☐ beam* | ☐ goal* | ☐ main | ☐ reach | ☐ tail* |
| ☐ bean* | ☐ goat* | ☐ mean* | ☐ read* | ☐ teach* |
| ☐ beat* | ☐ heap* | ☐ meat | ☐ real* | ☐ team* |
| ☐ beet | ☐ heat* | ☐ meet* | ☐ road* | ☐ toad* |
| ☐ boat* | ☐ heel* | ☐ nail | ☐ sail | ☐ wait* |
| ☐ coal* | ☐ jail | ☐ neat | ☐ seal* | ☐ weak |
| ☐ coat* | ☐ jeep | ☐ need* | ☐ seam | ☐ week* |
| ☐ deal* | ☐ keep* | ☐ pail | ☐ seat | ☐ weed |
| ☐ deed | ☐ lead* | ☐ pain* | ☐ seed* | ☐ weep |
| ☐ deep* | ☐ leak* | ☐ peach* | ☐ seek | |

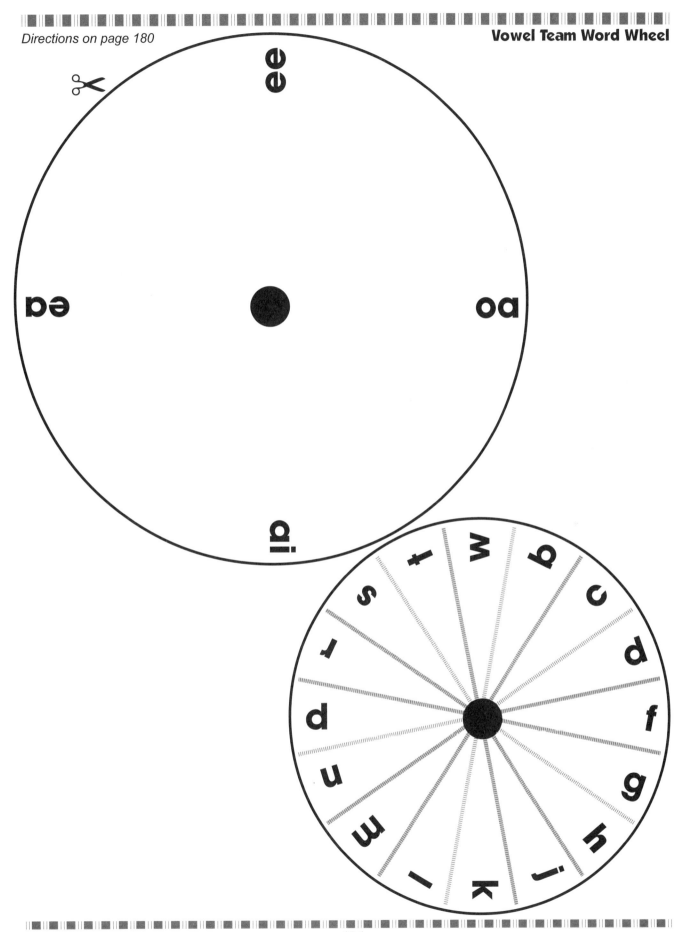

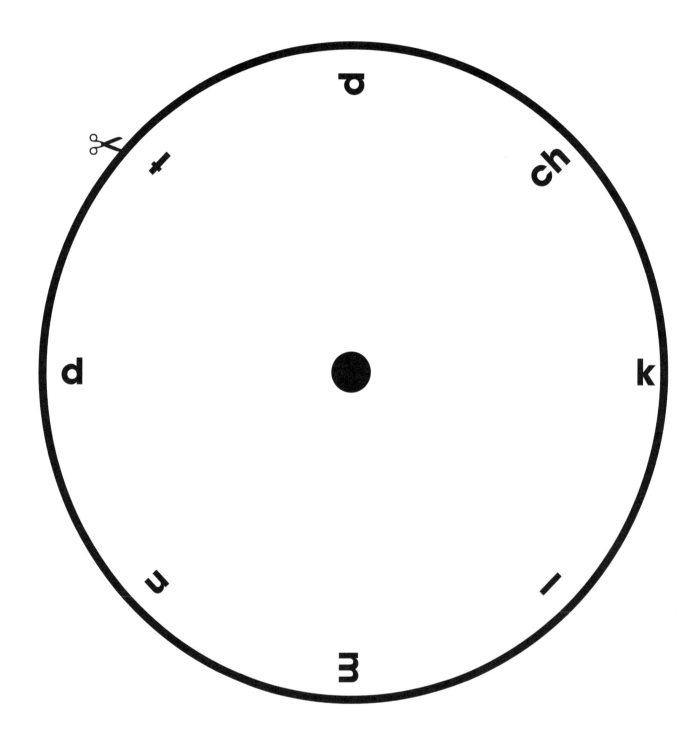

# Word Sort: Drive for Nine!

**Getting Ready to Play:** Copy the word cards on page 184 onto colorful card stock for each pair of students.

**Directions:**
1. Students are to cut out the cards along the dashed lines and then practice reading the words aloud with their partners.
2. Have students sort the set of words into two groups. For example, the two groups of words can be formed by using long vowel sounds as the categories. Invite students to think of another way to sort the words, too.

# Bingo Game: Drive for Nine!

**Getting Ready:** Make copies of the bingo boards on pages 185–187 on colorful card stock for each group of six students. Cut apart the boards along the dashed lines. To prepare the calling cards, copy page 184 onto card stock for each group and cut out the word cards. Give each student nine markers to place on the bingo board.

**How to Play:** Shuffle the word cards. Choose someone to be the "caller." One at a time, the caller announces the word. Each time a student hears a word that is shown on her board, she covers that space with a marker. The first player to cover all squares on his board calls out "Nine are mine!" and is declared the winner.

# Path Game: Space Race

**Getting Ready:** For each group of two or three players, you will need a set of word cards, game board, small game marker for each player, and die. Copy the game materials on pages 188 and 189 onto card stock. Cut apart the word cards along the dashed lines. Decorate the game board as desired with markers.

**How to Play:**
1. Shuffle the word cards and place them facedown in a stack.
2. Each player puts a marker on the Start space.
3. The first player draws a card and turns it face up. If the player reads the word correctly, he rolls the die, moves the number of spaces indicated, keeps the word card, and then passes the die to the next player. If the word is not read correctly, the card is placed in the discard pile. The second player now takes a turn.
4. The game continues until one player lands on the Finish space and is declared the winner.

| | | | | | |
|---|---|---|---|---|---|
| shake | grape | price | mile | ripe | dive |
| cake | ape | mice | pile | pipe | drive |
| stage | lane | wave | hike | pine | bite |
| cage | plane | gave | bike | dine | kite |
| race | name | gate | ride | dime | tire |
| face | game | skate | hide | chime | fire |

# Drive for Nine!

Bingo Board #2

| stage | kite | hide |
| --- | --- | --- |
| gave | ape | drive |
| ripe | chime | gate |

# Drive for Nine!

Bingo Board #1

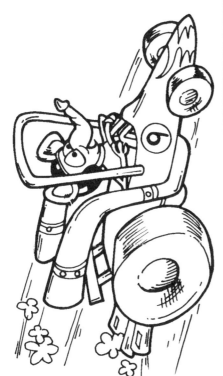

| grape | fire | pile |
| --- | --- | --- |
| lane | face | kite |
| pipe | dime | skate |

Directions on page 183

## Drive for Nine!
Bingo Board #4

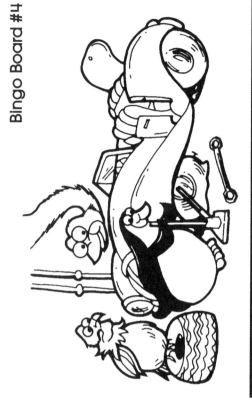

| mice | tire | hike |
| skate | ape | bike |
| pine | wave name | wave |

## Drive for Nine!
Bingo Board #3

| lane | bite | ride |
| mile | cage | wave |
| dine | ripe | gave |

## Drive for Nine!

Bingo Board #6

| fire | dive | mile |
| --- | --- | --- |
| race | shake | plane |
| name | cake | price |

## Drive for Nine!

Bingo Board #5

| game | gate | bike |
| --- | --- | --- |
| pile | cake | drive |
| dine | race | mice |

| | | | | | |
|---|---|---|---|---|---|
| beach | read | steam | leap | coal | oat |
| race | lead | zeal | treat | croak | goat |
| trace | bead | weak | heap | soak | float |
| space | teach | speak | mean | oak | coat |
| place | reach | sneak | clean | toad | boat |
| pace | peach | creak | cream | road | goal |
| lace | each | beak | beam | load | foal |

Space Race

Finish

Start

Directions on page 183

# More Little Words
## Variant Vowel, Diphthong, and *R*-Controlled Phonograms

| **-air** | **-all** | **-ar** | **-ard** | **-ark** | **-arm** | **-art** |
|---|---|---|---|---|---|---|
| air* | all* | car* | card* | bark* | arm* | cart |
| chair* | ball | far* | hard* | dark | farm | chart |
| fair | call* | jar* | yard | mark | harm | dart |
| hair* | fall | star* | | park* | | part* |
| pair | hall | | | | | smart |
| stair | mall | | | | | start* |
| | tall | | | | | |
| | wall* | | | | | |

| **-aw** | **-ay** | **-e** | **-ear** | **-ew** | **-ie** | **-ir** |
|---|---|---|---|---|---|---|
| caw* | bay* | be* | clear | blew | die | fir |
| claw | day* | he* | dear | chew | lie* | sir* |
| draw | hay* | me* | ear* | dew | pie* | stir |
| jaw* | jay* | she* | fear | few* | tie* | |
| law* | lay* | we* | near | flew | | |
| paw* | may* | | | grew | | |
| raw* | pay* | **-ee** | | new* | | **-ird** |
| saw* | play | bee* | | | | bird* |
| | ray* | fee | | | | third* |
| | say* | see* | | | | |
| | stay | tree | | | | |
| | way* | wee* | | | | |

| **-irl** | **-o** | **-oil** | **-oo** | **-ood** | **-ook** | **-ool** |
|---|---|---|---|---|---|---|
| girl | do* | boil | boo* | good* | book* | cool* |
| twirl | to* | oil* | coo | stood* | cook | pool* |
| | two | soil | goo | wood | hook | spool |
| | who* | | moo* | | look | stool |
| **-irt** | | | shoo | | shook | |
| dirt* | **-o** | | too* | | took* | |
| shirt* | go* | | zoo | | | |
| skirt | no* | | | | | |
| | so* | | | | | |

*The word is already printed on a card. (See pages 197–204.)*

| -oom | -oon | -oop | -or | -orn | -ort | -ouse |
|------|------|------|-----|------|------|-------|
| boom | loon | hoop | for* | born | fort* | blouse |
| bloom | moon* | loop | or* | corn* | port | house* |
| broom | noon | snoop | | horn* | short* | mouse* |
| room* | soon* | swoop | **-ork** | worn | sort | |
| zoom* | spoon | | cork* | | sport | |
| | | | fork* | | | |
| | | | pork | | | |

| -out | -ow | -ow | -own | -ur | | -y |
|------|-----|-----|------|-----|---|-----|
| out* | cow* | blow* | brown | fur* | by* | shy* |
| pout* | how* | crow | clown | blur | dry* | sky* |
| shout* | now* | glow | crown | | fly* | spy* |
| snout | plow | mow* | down | **-url** | fry* | try* |
| stout | pow | row* | drown | curl | my* | why* |
| | vow | show | frown | hurl | | |
| | wow | slow | town | | | |
| | | snow* | | | | |

**-oy**
boy*
joy*
toy*

## Other Little Words

| | | | |
|---|---|---|---|
| age* | eel*[3] | its* | owl* |
| ago* | egg* | key* | own* |
| am*[1] | elf*[2] | oak* | put* |
| an*[1] | eye* | oar* | tea* |
| and*[2] | gas | oat*[3] | the* |
| any* | has* | of* | they |
| are* | her* | off* | two |
| ask | hi* | oh* | was* |
| ate*[3] | ill*[2] | old*[3] | yak |
| buy* | in*[1] | one* | yes |
| eat*[3] | inn* | our* | you* |

*The word is already printed on a card.
  (See pages 197–204.)
[1]The word family is provided in the list
  on pages 42 and 43.
[2]The word family is provided in the list
  on pages 118 and 119.
[3]The word family is provided in the list
  on pages 158 and 159.

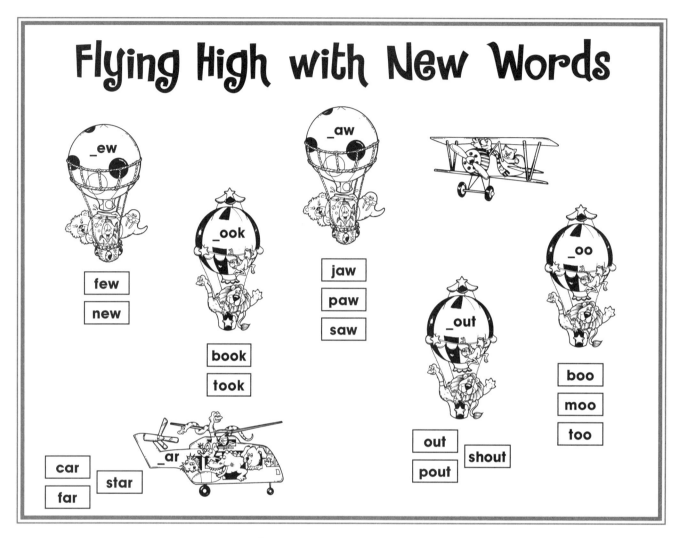

# Bulletin-Board Word Wall

**Getting Ready:** You will need sky-blue butcher paper, card stock, markers, scissors, stapler, and patterns on pages 193–204.

**Directions:**
1. Begin by covering the bulletin board with paper. Arrange the paper so that the top of this display can be reached by standing children if you would like them to point to words.
2. Copy the title and decorative art on pages 193 and 194 onto card stock. You may prefer to enlarge the art before making the reproductions. (Copy the title at 125% to make the lowercase letters about 3 in. [8 cm] in height.) Color the art as desired with markers and then cut out the individual pieces along the dashed lines. Staple the title in the center of the top of the board and other pieces where desired.
3. Select the phonograms you will introduce and then make as many copies of the patterns on pages 195 and 196 on card stock as needed for displaying the word families. Also, copy the word cards on pages 197–204 onto card stock and cut them out.
4. Place all materials on a table by the board and then add the pieces to the display as new words are introduced during classroom activities.

# Flying

# Bug

# with

# High

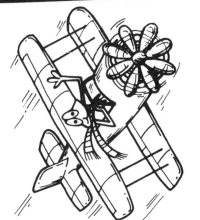

**193**

New Words

**194**

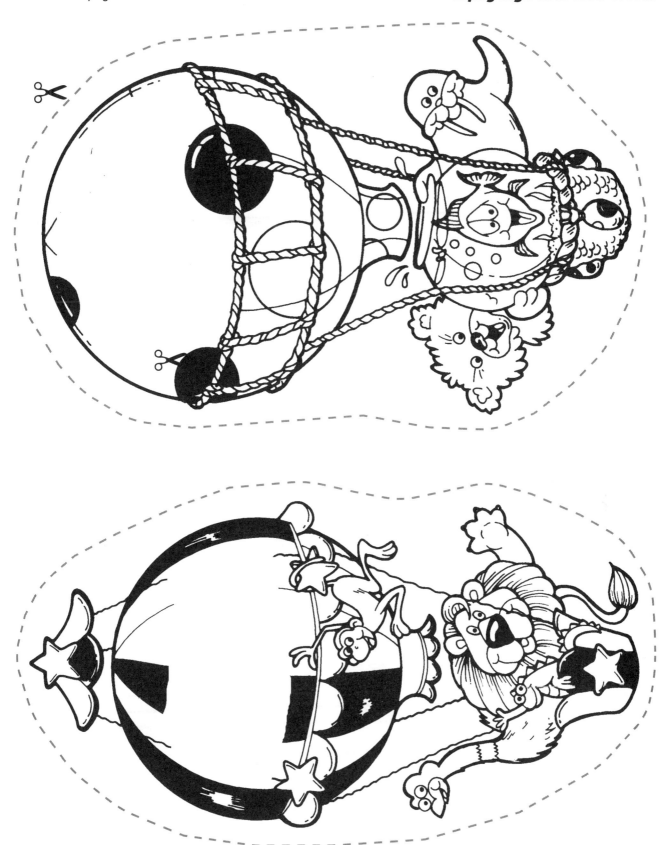

| age | ago | air |
| all | am | an |
| and | any | are |
| arm | ate | bay |
| be | bee | boo |
| boy | buy | by |

| car | caw | cow |
| --- | --- | --- |
| day | do | dry |
| ear | eat | eel |
| egg | elf | eye |
| far | few | fly |
| for | fry | fur |

| | | |
|---|---|---|
| go | hay | has |
| he | her | hi |
| how | ill | in |
| inn | its | jar |
| jay | jaw | joy |
| key | law | lay |

| lie | may | me |
|-----|-----|-----|
| moo | mow | my |
| new | no | now |
| oak | oar | oat |
| of | off | oh |
| oil | old | one |

| or | our | out |
|---|---|---|
| owl | own | paw |
| pay | pie | put |
| raw | ray | row |
| saw | say | see |
| she | shy | sir |

| sky | so | spy |
| --- | --- | --- |
| star | tea | the |
| tie | to | too |
| toy | try | was |
| way | we | wee |
| who | why | you |

| chair | hair | call |
|-------|------|------|
| wall | card | hard |
| bark | park | part |
| start | bird | third |
| dirt | shirt | good |
| stood | book | took |

| cool | pool | room |
| zoom | moon | soon |
| cork | fork | corn |
| horn | fort | short |
| house | mouse | pout |
| shout | blow | snow |

# We Can Spell

**Getting Ready:** You will need twelve 5" x 8" (13 cm x 20 cm) index cards and musical instrument, such as bells, rhythm sticks, or a tambourine. On each card, print one of the following words: *age\**, *ate\**, *bay\**, *day\**, *hay\**, *jay\**, *lay\**, *may\**, *pay\**, *ray\**, *say\**, and *way\**.

**Directions:** Teach students the song "We Can Spell," sung to the chorus of "Jingle Bells."

> *We can spell. We can spell.*
> *Spelling what we say.*
> *Oh, what fun it is to spell*
> *Some little words today.*

After singing the first verse, hold up a word card.
For example, show students the word *lay*.
Students respond:

> **L-a-y**, **l-a-y**,
> *Spelling the word* **lay**.
> *Oh, what fun it is to spell*
> *Some long* **a** *words today.*

After students learn the song, have them take turns using a musical instrument to accompany their singing.

**Culmination:** Select the words you would like to add to the "Flying High with New Words" bulletin-board word wall and print them on small index cards that have been cut in half. Label the word families on the appropriate shapes and include them with the words. (*Note*: Words above marked with an asterisk are provided on pages 197–202.)

# Sing and Spell with Double *L*

**Getting Ready:** On the board, list the following words in the *-all* family—*ball, call\*, fall, hall, mall, small, tall,* and *wall\**. Students may also review other double *L* words (*-ell, -ill,* and *-ull* word families) that were introduced on page 141.

**Directions:** Teach students "The Double *L* Song," sung to the chorus of "Jingle Bells."

> *Double* **L**'s
> *Double* **L**'s
> *We spell with double* **L**'s.
> *Oh, what fun it is to spell*
> *Words that end with* **L**'s.

For each additional verse, point to a double *L* word on the board, such as the word *ball*. Then, have the students sing the song.

> **B-a-l-l, b-a-l-l,**
> **B-a-l-l—ball**.
> *Oh, what fun it is to spell*
> *Words that end with* **L**'s.

Repeat the song with other double *L* words as time and interest allow.

**Culmination:** Follow the directions in the previous activity for the bulletin-board word wall.

# For *A's* a Jolly Good Letter

**Getting Ready:** On the board, list the following words—*age\*, ago\*, air\*, am\*, an\*, and\*, any\*, are\*, ask, ate\*, bay\*, car\*, caw\*, day\*, far\*, hay\*, jar\*, jaw\*, jay\*, lay\*, may\*, paw\*, pay\*, raw\*, ray\*, saw\*, say\*, star\*, was\*,* and *way\*.*

**Directions:**
1. Introduce the long *a* sound by telling students that sometimes the vowel *A* represents the sound like its name. Review VC*e* words (*age*). In addition, look for the vowel digraph *ay* in words listed on the board and underline that letter pair.
2. Teach students the song "For *A's* a Jolly Good Letter," sung to the tune of "For He's a Jolly Good Fellow." On the last line of the song, insert one of the words shown on the board. Students respond to the question by shaking their heads for *No* or nodding to signal *Yes* (*age, ate, bay, day, hay, jay, lay, may, pay, ray, say, way*).

   *For **A**'s a jolly good letter, for **A**'s a jolly good letter,*
   *For **A**'s a jolly good letter, sometimes it says its name.*
   *Sometimes it says its name. Sometimes it says its name.*
   *For **A**'s a jolly good letter, for **A**'s a jolly good letter,*
   *For **A**'s a jolly good letter, in **age** does it say its name?*

**Culmination:** Select the words you would like to add to the "Flying High with New Words" bulletin-board word wall and print them on small index cards that have been cut in half. Label the word families on the appropriate shapes and include them with the words. (*Note:* Words above marked with an asterisk are provided on pages 197–202.)

# For *E's* a Jolly Good Letter

**Getting Ready:** On the board, list the following words: *be\*, bee\*, ear\*, eat\*, eel\*, egg\*, elf\*, eye\*, few\*, key\*, lie\*, me\*, new\*, see\*, she\*, tea\*, the\*, we\*,* and *wee\*.* Also, include the words *blew, dew, few\*, flew,* and *grew.*

**Directions:**
1. Introduce the long *e* sound by telling students that sometimes the vowel *E* represents the sound like its name. Look for the vowel digraphs *ee, ea,* and *ey* in words listed on the board. Underline those letter clusters in the words. Be sure to compare the words *eye* and *key* to help students understand how those words are different.
2. Teach students the song "For *E's* a Jolly Good Letter," sung to the tune of "For He's a Jolly Good Fellow." (Refer to the lyrics above for the entire song.) On the last line of the song, insert one of the words shown on the board. Students respond by shaking their heads for *No* or nodding to signal *Yes* (*be, bee, ear, eat, eel, key, me, see, she, tea, we, wee*).

   *For **E**'s a jolly good letter, for **E**'s a jolly good letter,*
   *For **E**'s a jolly good letter; sometimes it says its name. . . .*

**Culmination:** Follow the directions in the previous activity for the bulletin-board word wall.

# Living Word Sort: Sounds for A

**Getting Ready:** Students have learned the long- and short-vowel sounds represented by the letter *A*. Introduce two more vowel sounds by listing the categories as illustrated below on chart paper. Copy the pictures on page 208 and 209 onto card stock. Cut out the pictures along the dashed lines for traditional card shapes or along the heavy black outline to make shaped cards. On each 5" x 8" (13 cm x 20 cm) index card, write one of the following words: *all, am\*, an\*, and\*, arm\*, ate\*, ball, bay\*, call\*, day\*, far\*, hay\*, jar\*, jay\*, lay\*, law\*, may\*, play, say\*, star\*,* and *wall\*.*

| | | | |
|---|---|---|---|
| 1. cat (/kăt/) | 2. gate (/gāt/) | 3. car (/kär/) | 4. ball (/bôl/) |

**Directions:** Introduce the four picture cards and then choose students to hold them in front of the class. One at a time, name each word on the word cards and have students listen for the sound of A. Then, choose a student to stand with the word card near the picture whose name has the same vowel sound. Continue until all word cards have been sorted by vowel sounds.

**Optional:** Tape the picture cards to the labeled chart paper. As each word is read, have students indicate which vowel sound they hear with a show of fingers for the number of the correct category listed on the chart. Then, write the word below the corresponding picture. Later, choose students to look for phonograms in the words, such as *-ar* and *-all*, and underline them. If you are interested in repeating this activity, refer to pages 42, 82, 118, 158, and 190 for additional words (short *a*, long *a*, and *r*-controlled sounds).

**Culmination:** Select the words you would like to add to the "Flying High with Words" bulletin-board word wall and print them on small index cards that have been cut in half. Label the word families on the appropriate shapes and include them with the words. (*Note:* Words above marked with an asterisk are provided on pages 197–202.)

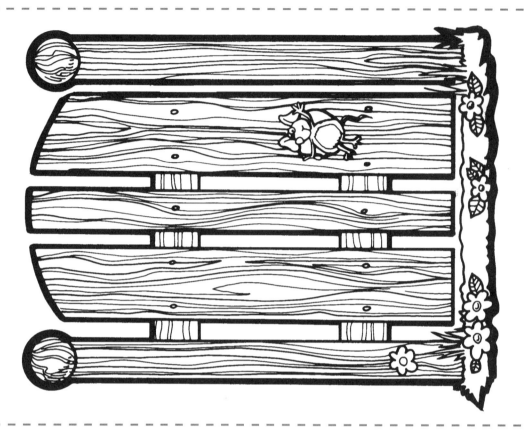

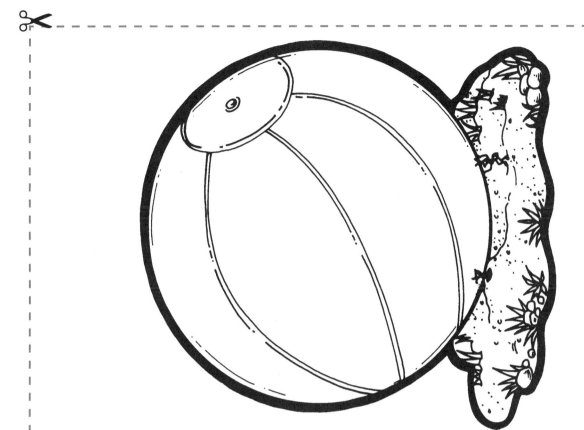

# Are You Thinking?

**Getting Ready:** On each 5" x 8" (13 cm x 20 cm) index card, print one of the following words: *bee\**, *eat\**, *eel\**, *egg\**, *key\**, *see\**, *she\**, *tea\**, *the\**, and *wee\**. In addition, list the words on the board.

**Directions:** Review the long *e* sound with students. Read aloud the words printed on the board and identify those that have the long *e* sound. Teach students the song "Are You Thinking?" sung to the tune of "Frère Jacques." Place the word cards facedown in your lap. Hold up one card while you sing the first part of the verse. Place the card facedown again as students respond by the "spelling" the word. For example, show the word *see* and then sing the song:

Teacher sings:  *Are you thinking?*
  *Are you thinking?*
  *Please spell* **see**.
  *Please spell* **see**.
Students sing:  *Spelling* **see** *is easy.*
  *Spelling* **see** *is easy.*
  **S-e-e**.
  **S-e-e**.

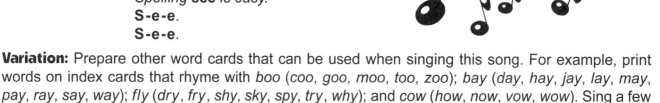

**Variation:** Prepare other word cards that can be used when singing this song. For example, print words on index cards that rhyme with *boo* (*coo, goo, moo, too, zoo*); *bay* (*day, hay, jay, lay, may, pay, ray, say, way*); *fly* (*dry, fry, shy, sky, spy, try, why*); and *cow* (*how, now, vow, wow*). Sing a few words each day to reinforce how to spell these itty-bitty words.

**Culmination:** Select the words you would like to add to the "Flying High with New Words" bulletin-board word wall and print them on small index cards that have been cut in half. Label the word families on the appropriate shapes and include them with the words. (*Note*: Words above marked with an asterisk are provided on pages 197–202.)

# See and Say /ew/

**Getting Ready:** For each student, you will need 14 small index cards. On the board, print the following words: *bee\**, *blew*, *chew*, *dew*, *eel\**, *eye\**, *few\**, *flew*, *grew*, *pie\**, *the\**, *they*, *tie\** and *yes*. In addition, list the words on the board.

**Directions:**
1. Have students write one of the words on each index card.
2. Read aloud the words on the board in random order. Ask, "What vowel sound do you hear?" after reading each word.
3. As you name the words, have students hold up the correct word cards. If they hear the /ew/ sound, invite them to respond by saying that sound very dramatically and then set aside that word in a separate pile.
4. Have students choose four *-ew* word cards. Direct them to fold sheets of paper into four equal sections. In each section, students print one of selected *-ew* words, use it correctly in a sentence that starts with the word *Yesterday*, and illustrate the sentence with markers.

**Culmination:** Follow the directions in the previous activity for the bulletin-board word wall.

# See Y—Say I

**Getting Ready:** For each student, you will need 11 small index cards. On the board, print the following words—*buy\*, by\*, dry\*, fly\*, fry\*, my\*, shy\*, sky\*, spy\*, try\*,* and *why\**.

**Directions:**

1. Have students write one of the words on each index card.
2. Read aloud the words, one at a time, on the board in random order. Ask, "What sound do you hear at the end of the word?"
3. As you name the words, have students hold up the correct word cards. Practice until they can hold up the appropriate cards instantly.
4. Direct students to fold a sheet of paper into four equal sections. In each section, have them print a word that ends with the letter *Y* that stands for the long *i* sound and then draw a picture for the word.

**Culmination:** Select the words you would like to add to the "Flying High with New Words" bulletin-board word wall and print them on small index cards that have been cut in half. Label the word family on the appropriate shape and include it with the words. (*Note*: Words above marked with an asterisk are provided on pages 197–202.)

# Living Word Sort: Sounds for I

**Getting Ready:** Copy the pictures on page 212 onto card stock. Cut out the pictures along the dashed lines. On each 5" x 8" (13 cm x 20 cm) index card, write one of the following words: *hi\*, ill\*, inn\*, its\*, lie\*, pie\*,* and *tie\**.

**Directions:** Introduce the picture cards by reviewing the short *i* sound as in the word *fish* and the long *i* sound as in the word *mice*. Give the two picture cards to students to hold in front of the group. Name each word on the words cards and have students indicate which vowel sound they hear. Then, choose a student to hold the word card near the picture  whose name has the same vowel sound. For example, the word *pie* has a long *i* sound. The child holding the word card should stand near the picture of mice to be correct. Continue this procedure until all word cards have been sorted by vowel sounds.

**Optional:** Tape the picture cards to chart paper. As each word is read, have students indicate which vowel sound they hear. Then, write the word under the corresponding picture. If you are interested in repeating this activity, refer to pages 43, 82, 119, and 159 for additional words. Also, have students practice reading words from the *-y* family (*by, dry, fly, fry, my, shy, sky, spy, try,* and *why*).

**Culmination:** Follow the directions in the previous activity for the bulletin-board word wall.

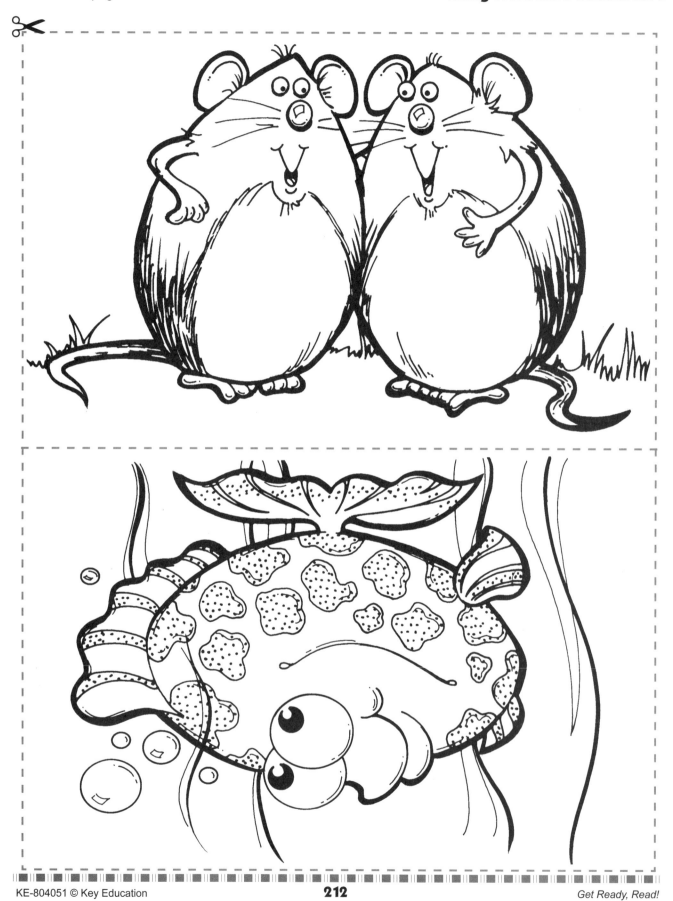

# Living Word Sort: Sounds for O

**Getting Ready:** Students have learned the short- and long-vowel sounds represented by the letter *O*. Introduce three more vowel sounds by listing the categories as illustrated below on chart paper. Copy the pictures on pages 214 and 215 and the cow on page 21 onto card stock. Cut out the pictures along the dashed lines. On each 5" x 8" (13 cm x 20 cm) index card, print one of the following words: *boo\*, boy\*, coo, cow\*, do\*, for\*, go\*, how\*, joy\*, moo\*, no\*, now\*, oh\*, old\*, our\*, out\*, owl\*, own\*, so\*, to\*, too\*, toy\*, two, who\*,* and *zoo.*

| 1. lock (/lŏk/) | 2. boat (/bōt/) | 3. moon (/mo͞on/) | 4. boy (/boi/) | 5. cow (/kou/) |
|---|---|---|---|---|

**Directions:** Introduce the five picture cards and then choose students to hold them in front of the class. One at a time, name each word on the word cards and have students listen for the vowel sound. Then, choose a student to stand with the word card near the picture whose name has the same vowel sound. Continue until all word cards have been sorted by vowel sounds.

**Optional:** Tape the picture cards to the labeled chart paper. As each word is read, have students indicate which vowel sound they hear with a show of fingers for the number of the correct category listed on the chart. Then, write the word below the corresponding picture. Later, choose students to look for phonograms in the words, such as *-oo, -ow,* and *-oy,* and underline them.

**Culmination:** Select the words you would like to add to the "Flying High with New Words" bulletin-board word wall and print them on small index cards that have been cut in half. Label the word families on the appropriate shapes and include them with the words. (*Note*: Words above marked with an asterisk are provided on pages 197–202.)

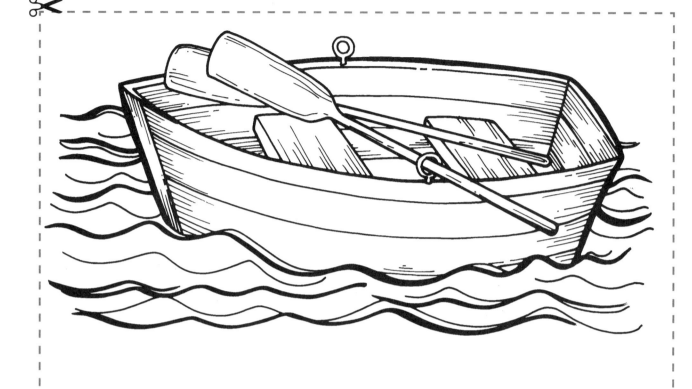

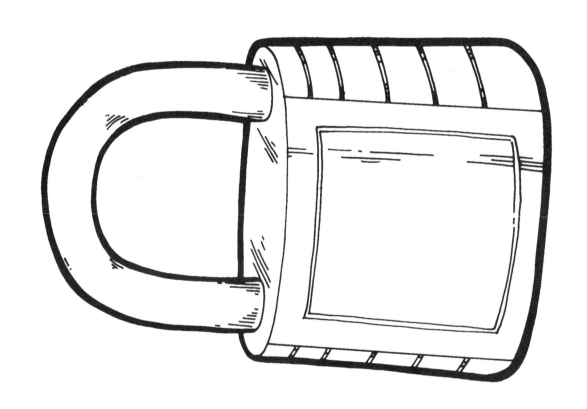

# Living Word Sort: -AY and -Y

**Getting Ready:** Copy the pictures on page 217 and 218 onto card stock. Cut out the pictures along the dashed lines. Set aside the picture of the ear of corn. On each 5" x 8" (13 cm x 20 cm) index card, print one of the following words: *bay\*, bird\*, by\*, car\*, day\*, dry\*, far\*, fly\*, fry\*, hay\*, jar\*, jay\*, lay\*, may\*, my\*, pay\*, play, ray\*, say\*, shy\*, sir\*, sky\*, star\*, third\*, try\*, way\*,* and *why\**. Print the categories for the word sort as illustrated below on chart paper.

| 1. long *a* sound (cake) | 2. long *i* sound ("fly" as an action) | 3. Other words (trash can) |
| --- | --- | --- |

**Directions:** Introduce the three picture cards and explain that the cake represents the long *a* sound and fly as an action represents the long *i* sound. The trash can is for those words that do not belong in either of the other two categories. Give the three pictures to students to hold in front of the class. One at a time, name each word on the cards and have students indicate which long vowel sound they hear with a show of fingers for the number of the correct category on the chart. Choose a student to stand with the word card near the corresponding picture. Continue until all word cards have been sorted by vowel sounds.

**Culmination:** Select the words you would like to add to the "Flying High with New Words" bulletin-board word wall and print them on small index cards that have been cut in half. Label the word families on the appropriate shapes and include them with the words. (*Note*: Words above marked with an asterisk are provided on pages 197–204.)

# Living Word Sort: *R*-Controlled Sounds

**Getting Ready:** Copy the pictures on page 217 and 218 onto card stock. Cut out the pictures along the dashed lines. Set aside the picture of the cake. On each 5" x 8" (13 cm x 20 cm) index card, print one of the following words: *bird\*, born, blur, cork\*, corn\*, curl, fir, for\*, fork\*, fort\*, fur\*, girl, horn\*, hurl, or\*, pork, port, sir\*, short\*, sport, stir, third\*, twirl,* and *worn*. Other words to include (these will be "dropped" into the trash can): *boy\*, joy\*, lie\*, pie\*, tie\*,* and *toy\**. Print the categories for the word sort as illustrated below on chart paper.

| 1. /ûr/ (bird) | 2. /ôr/ (corn) | 3. Other words (trash can) |
| --- | --- | --- |

**Directions:** Introduce the three picture cards and explain that in words the letter clusters *ir* and *ur* stand for the vowel sound as in *bird*. Words with the letter cluster *or* have the vowel sound as in *corn*. The trash can is for those words that do not belong in either of the other two categories. Give the three pictures to students to hold in front of the class. One at a time, name each word on the cards and have students indicate which long vowel sound they hear with a show of fingers for the number of the correct category on the chart. Choose a student to stand with the word card near the corresponding picture. Continue until all word cards have been sorted by vowel sounds.

**Culmination:** Follow the directions in the previous activity for the bulletin-board word wall.

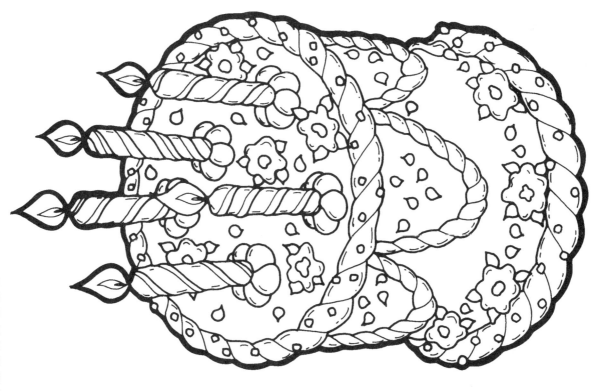

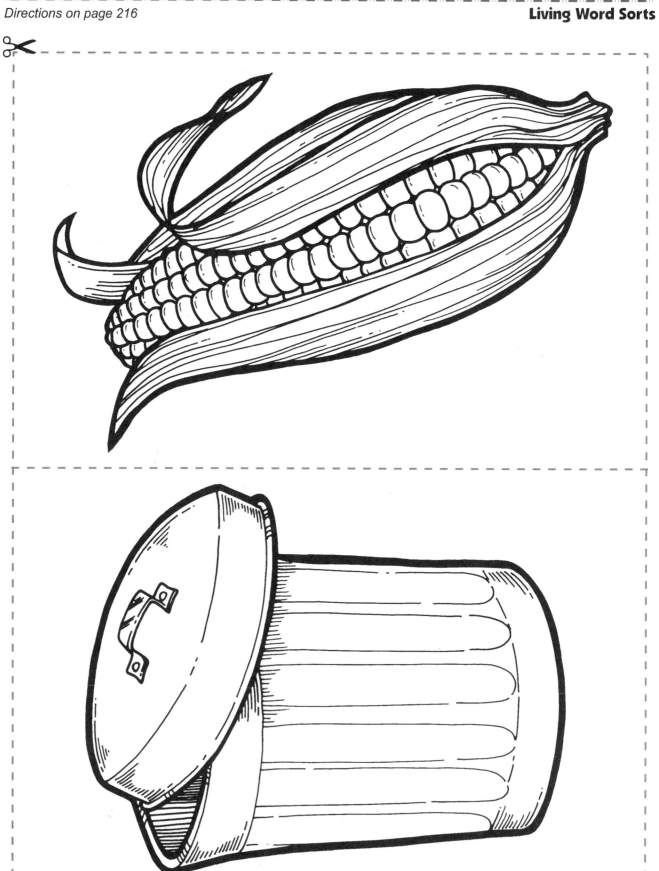

# Changing One Letter

**Directions:** Have students write the numbers 1–10 on their papers. One at a time, print a word (words listed below) on the board and then provide the directions for changing it into a new word. Have students record the new words on their papers. Choose a student to name each new word and list the correct answers on the board.

## Set A
1. car*—Change one letter to spell card*.
2. by*—Change one letter to spell bay*.
3. moo*—Change one letter to spell coo.
4. cow*—Change one letter to spell caw*.
5. boo*—Change one letter to spell too*.
6. boy*—Change one letter to spell toy*.
7. pie*—Change one letter to spell lie*.
8. jay*—Change one letter to spell jaw*.
9. blew—Change one letter to spell blow*.
10. who*—Change one letter to spell why*.

## Set B
1. age*—Change one letter to spell ago*.
2. and*—Change one letter to spell any*.
3. are*—Change one letter to spell ate*.
4. day*—Change one letter to spell dry*.
5. far*—Change one letter to spell for*.
6. fly*—Change one letter to spell fry*.
7. law*—Change one letter to spell lay*.
8. new*—Change one letter to spell now*.
9. the*—Change one letter to spell tie*.
10. arm*—Change one letter to spell farm.

## Set C
1. crow—Change one letter to spell cow*.
2. room*—Change one letter to spell broom.
3. sort—Change one letter to spell short*.
4. few*—Change one letter to spell flew.
5. spoon—Change one letter to spell soon*.
6. pork—Change one letter to spell park*.
7. caw*—Change one letter to spell claw.
8. spy*—Change one letter to spell say*.
9. way*—Change one letter to spell why*.
10. am*—Change one letter to spell arm*.

## Set D
1. pool*—Change one letter to spell spool.
2. shirt*—Change one letter to spell skirt.
3. slow—Change one letter to spell show.
4. row*—Change one letter to spell raw*.
5. crown—Change one letter to spell drown.
6. sky*—Change one letter to spell shy*.
7. my*—Change one letter to spell may*.
8. cart—Change one letter to spell chart.
9. snout—Change one letter to spell shout*.
10. show—Change one letter to spell snow*.

**Culmination:** Select the words you would like to add to the "Flying High with New Words" bulletin-board word wall and print them on small index cards that have been cut in half. Label the word families on the appropriate shapes and include them with the words. (*Note*: Words above marked with an asterisk are provided on pages 197–204.)

# Slip 'n' Spell Snail

**Getting Ready:** Copy the Slip 'n' Spell Snail and letter strips on pages 221 and 222 onto colorful card stock for each student. Copy the word cards on pages 222 and 223 onto card stock for each team of players and then cut apart the cards along the dashed lines. The words on page 222 are more difficult to spell and may be set aside if not appropriate for the children to use.

**Directions:**

1. Students are to decorate and cut out their own Slip 'n' Spell Snails. Also, have them cut out the paper strips.
2. Help students cut the six slits on their snails into which the letter strips will slide. Make sure they put the strips in order. (The strip for the final letter has three stars.)
3. To practice using the Slip 'n' Spell Snail, select a word from the list below and have students slide the strips to spell it. Continue in this manner as time and interest allow.

**How to Play:** Have students form groups of two or three players. Arrange the word cards facedown in a stack. The first player draws a card and reads the word for the second player to make on a Slip 'n' Spell Snail. If the second player spells the word correctly, she collects the word card. That player then draws a card for the third player to spell. Have students play the game for a predetermined length of time.

---

## Slip 'n' Spell Word List

### Examples include the following words:

**b:** bad, bag, ban, bar, bark, bay, bed, bee, beet, beg, bib, bid, big, bin, bob, bog, boo, book, boom, born, bow, boy, bud, bug, bun, buy

**c:** can, cap, car, caw, cod, cop, coo, cook, cool, cork, corn, cow, cud, cup

**d:** dab, dad, day, den, deep, dew, did, die, dig, dim, dip, dog, dub, dug

**f:** fad, fan, far, fed, few, fib, fig, fin, fir, fog, for, fork, fur

**g:** gab, gag, gap, gas, gem, get, goo, good, gum, gut

**h:** had, hair, ham, has, hay, hen, her, hey, hid, him, hip, his, hog, hook, hop, horn, how, hub, hug, hum

**m:** mad, main, man, map, mar, may, meet, men, met, mew, mom, moo, moon, mop, mow, mud, mug

**n:** nab, nail, nag, nap, net, new, nib, nip, nod, noon, nor, not, now

**p:** pad, pail, pain, pair, pan, paw, pay, peg, peek, peep, pen, pep, pet, pod, pool, pork, pop, pow, pug, pup

**r:** rag, rain, ram, ran, rap, raw, ray, red, rib, rid, rig, rim, rip, rob, rod, row, rub, run

**s:** sad, sag, sail, sap, saw, say, see, seed, seek, sip, sir, sob, son, soon, sub, sum, sun

**t:** tab, tag, tail, ten, tin, tip, too, took, toy, tub, tug

---

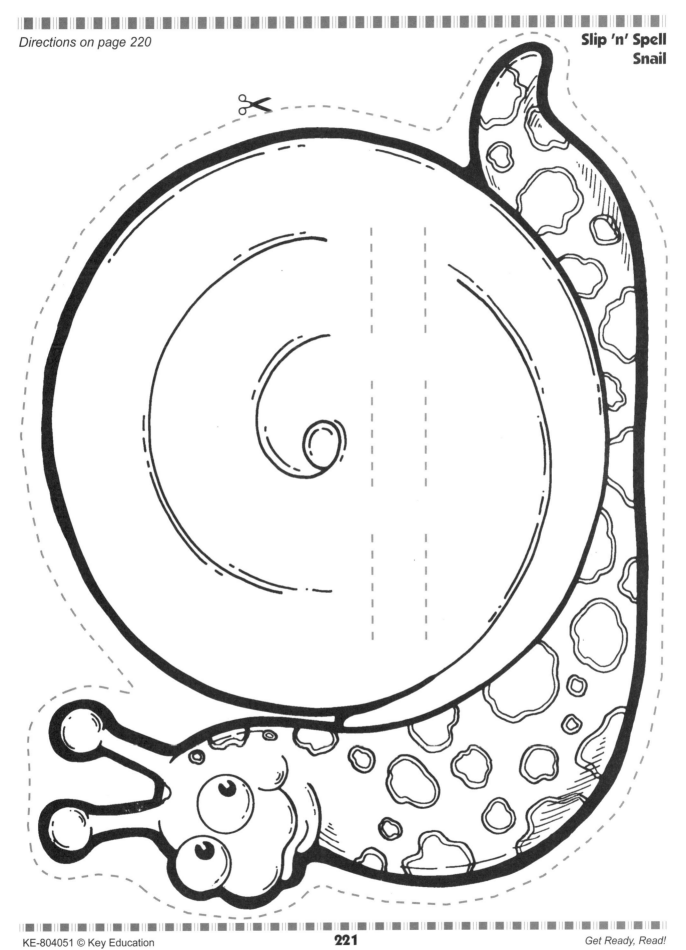

| | | |
|---|---|---|
| b | a | b |
| c | e | d |
| d | i | g |
| f | o | k |
| g | u | l |
| h | | m |
| m | ai | n |
| n | ar | p |
| p | ee | r |
| r | oo | s |
| s | or | w |
| t | | y |
| ★ | ★★ | ★★★ |
| **Slip 'n'** | **Slip 'n'** | **Slip 'n'** |
| **Spell—Snail** | **Spell—Snail** | **Spell—Snail** |

| | | |
|---|---|---|
| peek | book | horn |
| pair | good | corn |
| hair | cook | fork |
| rain | meet | part |
| tail | deep | bark |
| sail | seek | moon |

| | | | | | | |
|---|---|---|---|---|---|---|
| cow | hug | mud | pug | row | see | tug |
| coo | how | mow | pow | rig | say | tub |
| caw | hey | mop | pay | red | saw | toy |
| car | his | moo | paw | ray | sat | too |
| boo | her | may | now | raw | sag | ten |
| bow | dew | goo | new | rag | sad | sob |

# Making Little Words

**Getting Ready:** For each group of three or four students, copy the Word Maker slips below and on page 225. Using a paper cutter, cut apart the long strips on the horizontal dashed lines. Then, use scissors to cut apart the individual word slips. Put each set of slips in a lunch bag.

**How to Play:** To review three-letter words, divide the class into groups of three or four students. Give each group a bag of word slips. The first student draws a slip and tries to make a word by writing a vowel between the letters. If the other players agree that a word has been made, the first player keeps the slip. If not, the slip is placed in the discard pile. The second player then draws a word slip. The game continues until a predetermined time. The player with the most word slips is declared the winner.

**Optional:** Give each student a copy of the Word Maker pages that have not been cut apart. Challenge students to fill in their copies to make as many words as possible in five minutes.

| b _ b | b _ g | b _ g | b _ n |
| b _ y | c _ b | c _ d | c _ n |
| c _ t | d _ b | d _ d | d _ g |
| d _ m | d _ n | d _ p | d _ y |
| f _ b | f _ g | f _ n | f _ n |
| f _ n | f _ r | f _ t | f _ x |
| g _ b | g _ s | g _ t | g _ t |
| h _ d | h _ m | h _ p | h _ r |
| h _ s | h _ t | h _ t | j _ g |
| j _ m | j _ y | j _ y | l _ b |

| | | | |
|---|---|---|---|
| l _ d | l _ g | l _ p | l _ t |
| l _ w | l _ y | m _ d | m _ d |
| m _ g | m _ n | m _ n | m _ p |
| m _ t | m _ x | n _ d | n _ p |
| n _ t | n _ w | n _ w | p _ d |
| p _ g | p _ n | p _ n | p _ t |
| p _ y | r _ b | r _ d | r _ g |
| r _ n | r _ n | r _ p | r _ t |
| r _ w | r _ y | s _ d | s _ g |
| s _ n | s _ p | s _ t | s _ w |
| s _ y | t _ b | t _ g | t _ n |
| t _ n | t _ p | t _ p | v _ t |
| w _ g | w _ n | w _ s | w _ t |
| y _ k | y _ m | y _ s | y _ t |

# Three Word-Sort Activities

**Activity 1:** Use page 227.
**Activity 2:** Use page 231.
**Activity 3:** Use page 235.

**Getting Ready:** Copy the word cards on pages 227, 231, and 235 onto colorful card stock for each pair of students.

**Directions:**
1. Students are to cut out the cards along the dashed lines and then practice reading the words aloud with their partners.
2. Direct students to sort each set of words in different ways. For example in Activity 1, two groups of words can be formed by using the long *a* sound (*hay*, *air*) and the broad *a* sound (*ball*, *law*) as categories.

# Three Bingo Games

**All Paws on Play! Bingo Game:** Use pages 227–230.
**Come, Blow Your Horn Bingo Game:** Use pages 231–234.
**Shooting a Few Hoops Bingo Game:** Use pages 235–238.

**Getting Ready:** Make copies of the bingo boards (pages 228–230, 232–234, or 236–238) onto colorful card stock for each group of six students. Cut apart the boards along the dashed lines. To prepare the calling cards, copy page 227, 231, or 235 onto card stock for each group and cut out the word cards. Give each student nine markers to place on the bingo board.

**How to Play:** Shuffle the word cards. Choose someone to be the "caller." One at a time, the caller announces the word. Each time a student hears a word that is shown on her board, she covers that space with a marker. The first player to cover all squares on his board calls out the title of the game and is declared the winner.

# Path Game: Around the Barnyard

**Getting Ready:** For each group of two or three players, you will need a set of word cards, game board, standard die, and small game marker for each player. Copy pages 197–202 onto colorful card stock and cut out the cards along the dashed lines. Also, copy the game board on page 239 onto card stock and decorate it as desired with markers.

**How to Play:** Shuffle the word cards and place them facedown in a stack. Each player puts a marker on the Start space. The first player draws a card and reads the word. If the player reads the word correctly, he rolls the die, moves the number of spaces indicated, keeps the word card, and then passes the die to the next player. If the word is not read correctly, the card is placed in the discard pile. If the game marker lands on a picture of an animal, the player must spell that animal's name. If the spelling is correct, the player draws another word card to keep as a bonus. The second player now takes a turn. The game continues until 10 cards (or another predetermined number) have been collected by one of the players who is then declared the winner.

| | | | | | |
|---|---|---|---|---|---|
| small | jaw | day | play | stall | stair |
| mall | draw | bay | pay | all | pair |
| hall | claw | saw | may | way | hair |
| fall | caw | raw | lay | stay | fair |
| call | wall | paw | jay | say | chair |
| ball | tall | law | hay | ray | air |

*Directions on page 226*

## All Paws on Play!
Bingo Board #2

| | | |
|---|---|---|
| bay | paw | air |
| caw | ball | day |
| hay | fair | fall |

## All Paws on Play!
Bingo Board #1

| | | |
|---|---|---|
| claw | pair | small |
| day | saw | hair |
| hall | all | lay |

# All Paws on Play!
### Bingo Board #4

| fair | call | jaw |
| --- | --- | --- |
| jay | draw | stair |
| ball | mall | may |

# All Paws on Play!
### Bingo Board #3

| mall | raw | chair |
| --- | --- | --- |
| air | stall | tall |
| way | law | stay |

*Directions on page 226*

# All Paws on Play!

Bingo Board #6

| say | all | pair |
|-----|-----|------|
| stair | play | draw |
| tall | claw | small |

# All Paws on Play!

Bingo Board #5

| jaw | wall | pay |
|-----|------|-----|
| hair | saw | chair |
| ray | hall | stall |

| port | horn | vow | snow | crown | plow |
|------|------|-----|------|-------|------|
| fort | corn | pow | slow | brown | owl |
| for | born | now | show | town | row |
| pork | sport | how | glow | down | blow |
| fork | sort | cow | crow | drown | frown |
| cork | short | worn | wow | mow | clown |

*Directions on page 226*

# Come, Blow Your Horn

Bingo Board #2

| | | |
|---|---|---|
| crow | drown | fork |
| sport | wow | cow |
| town | port | corn |

✂ ─ ─ ─ ─ ─ ─ ─ ─ ─ ─ ─ ─ ─ ─ ─ ─ ─ ─ ─

# Come, Blow Your Horn

Bingo Board #1

| | | |
|---|---|---|
| snow | frown | cork |
| pow | how | row |
| owl | sort | born |

## Come, Blow Your Horn

Bingo Board #4

| down | mow | worn |
|------|------|------|
| clown | pork | blow |
| show | plow | fort |

## Come, Blow Your Horn

Bingo Board #3

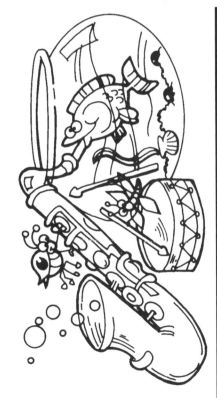

| blow | slow | brown |
|------|------|------|
| crown | for | vow |
| glow | now | horn |

# Come, Blow Your Horn

## Bingo Board #6

| cork | brown | horn |
|------|-------|------|
| how | sport | show |
| clown | cow | fort |

# Come, Blow Your Horn

## Bingo Board #5

| owl | short | frown |
|-----|-------|-------|
| down | glow | corn |
| fork | wow | row |

| grew | zoo | loon | room | book | stood |
| flew | moo | spool | boom | hoop | good |
| blew | goo | stool | soon | loop | took |
| new | coo | pool | noon | snoop | look |
| few | boo | cool | spoon | broom | hook |
| wood | stood | shoo | moon | zoom | cook |

## Shooting a Few Hoops

Bingo Board #2

| goo | look | grew |
|-----|------|------|
| hoop | zoom | stood |
| room | loop | soon |

## Shooting a Few Hoops

Bingo Board #1

| boom | took | boo |
|------|------|-----|
| stool | moon | hook |
| new | book | flew |

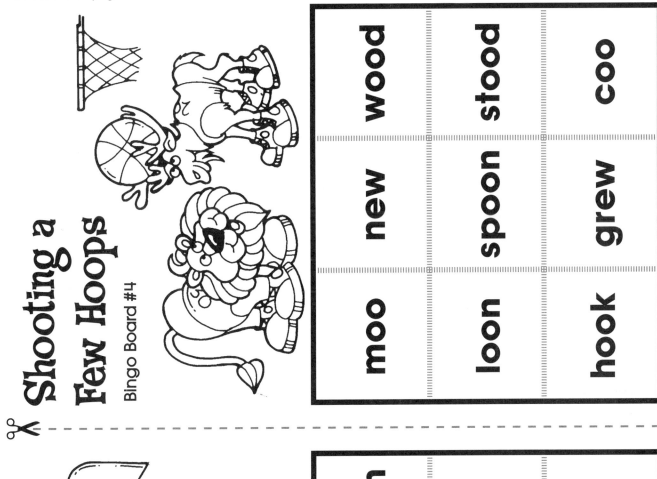

# Shooting a Few Hoops

Bingo Board #4

| wood | new | moo |
|------|-----|-----|
| stood | spoon | loon |
| coo | grew | hook |

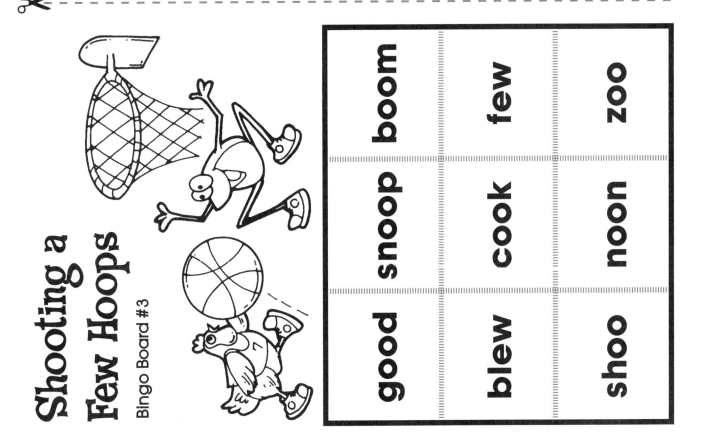

# Shooting a Few Hoops

Bingo Board #3

| boom | snoop | good |
|------|-------|------|
| few | cook | blew |
| zoo | noon | shoo |

# Shooting a Few Hoops

### Bingo Board #6

| | | |
|---|---|---|
| few | good | broom |
| stood | shoo | cool |
| book | blew | took |

# Shooting a Few Hoops

### Bingo Board #5

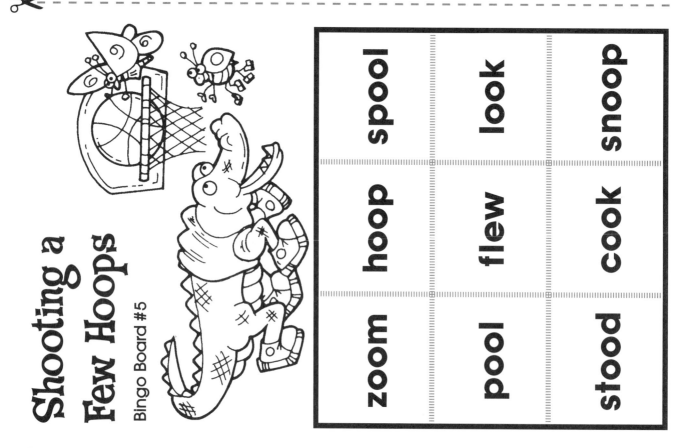

| | | |
|---|---|---|
| spool | hoop | zoom |
| look | flew | pool |
| snoop | cook | stood |

*Directions on page 226*

## Around the Barnyard

**Start**

*Get Ready, Read!*

# Correlations to NCTE/IRA Standards

*Get Ready, Read!* supports the *NCTE/IRA Standards for the English Language Arts* and the recommended teaching practices outlined in the NAEYC/IRA position statement *Learning to Read and Write: Developmentally Appropriate Practices for Young Children*.

## NCTE/IRA Standards for the English Language Arts

The activities in this book support the following standards:

1. **Students read many different types of print and nonprint texts for a variety of purposes.**
   Students must read both words and pictures in order to do the activities and games in *Get Ready, Read!*

2. **Students use a variety of strategies to build meaning while reading.**
   Activities and group lessons focusing on letter-sound relationships, word identification, phonemic awareness, and word families support this standard.

3. **Students communicate in spoken, written, and visual form for a variety of purposes and a variety of audiences.**
   In *Get Ready, Read!* students communicate verbally through group games, songs, and discussions; in writing as part of several activities; and visually through art projects.

4. **Students become participating members of a variety of literacy communities.**
   The many group activities in *Get Ready, Read!* help teachers build classroom literacy communities.

## NAEYC/IRA Position Statement *Learning to Read and Write: Developmentally Appropriate Practices for Young Children*

Each activity in this book supports one or more of the following recommended teaching practices for kindergarten and primary-grade students:

1. **Teachers provide balanced literacy instruction that incorporates systematic phonics instruction along with meaningful reading and writing activities.**
   *Get Ready, Read!* contains phonics activities that form an important part of balanced literacy instruction.

2. **Teachers provide opportunities for students to write many different kinds of texts for different purposes.**
   In *Get Ready, Read!* students write words to culminate activities and in response to dictation.

3. **Teachers provide opportunities for children to work in small groups.**
   *Get Ready, Read!* includes many small group activities.

4. **Teachers provide challenging instruction that expands children's knowledge of their world and expands their vocabularies.**
   The games, activities, and group lessons in *Get Ready, Read!* introduce and reinforce many vocabulary words.